Editor-in-Chief and Founder:
  Lyndon H. LaRouche, Jr.
Editorial Board: *Lyndon H. LaRouche, Jr. , Helga
  Zepp-LaRouche, Robert Ingraham, Tony
  Papert, Gerald Rose, Dennis Small, Jeffrey
  Steinberg, William Wertz*
Co-Editors: *Robert Ingraham, Tony Papert*
Technology: *Marsha Freeman*
Transcriptions: *Katherine Notley*
Ebooks: *Richard Burden*
Graphics: *Alan Yue*
Photos: *Stuart Lewis*
Circulation Manager: *Stanley Ezrol*

INTELLIGENCE DIRECTORS
Economics: *Marcia Merry Baker, Paul Gallagher*
History: *Anton Chaitkin*
Ibero-America: *Dennis Small*
Russia and Eastern Europe: *Rachel Douglas*
United States: *Debra Freeman*

INTERNATIONAL BUREAUS
Bogotá: *Miriam Redondo*
Berlin: *Rainer Apel*
Copenhagen: *Tom Gillesberg*
Lima: *Sara Madueño*
Melbourne: *Robert Barwick*
Mexico City: *Gerardo Castilleja Chávez*
New Delhi: *Ramtanu Maitra*
Paris: *Christine Bierre*
Stockholm: *Ulf Sandmark*
United Nations, N.Y.C.: *Leni Rubinstein*
Washington, D.C.: *William Jones*
Wiesbaden: *Göran Haglund*

ON THE WEB
e-mail: eirns@larouchepub.com
www.larouchepub.com
www.executiveintelligencereview.com
www.larouchepub.com/eiw
Webmaster: *John Sigerson*
Assistant Webmaster: *George Hollis*
Editor, Arabic-language edition: *Hussein Askary*

———————————————————————

EIR (ISSN 0273-6314) *is published weekly
(50 issues), by EIR News Service, Inc.,
P.O. Box 17390, Washington, D.C. 20041-0390.
(703) 297-8434*

European Headquarters: E.I.R. GmbH, Postfach
Bahnstrasse 9a, D-65205, Wiesbaden, Germany
Tel: 49-611-73650
Homepage: http://www.eir.de
e-mail: info@eir.de
Director: Georg Neudecker

Montreal, Canada: 514-461-1557
eir@eircanada.ca

Denmark: EIR - Danmark, Sankt Knuds Vej 11,
basement left, DK-1903 Frederiksberg, Denmark.
Tel.: +45 35 43 60 40, Fax: +45 35 43 87 57. e-mail:
eirdk@hotmail.com.

Mexico City: EIR, Sor Juana Inés de la Cruz 242-2
Col. Agricultura C.P. 11360
Delegación M. Hidalgo, México D.F.
Tel. (5525) 5318-2301
eirmexico@gmail.com

London Is Exposed and Vulnerable

Italy and Glass-Steagall Could Save Europe, The Threat Is from the City of London

May 22—The latest terrible "Russian threat" is now claimed to be coming from the two parties that have agreed to form a new government in Italy. Stalwarts of European stagnation and financial speculation are lining up to warn of the end of their world if the Lega and M5S (Five Star) parties' coalition is not prevented. We are supposed to forget that these parties were just favored by Italian voters for their policies, in elections held in March—just as we have been told for two years to forget that American voters, not Russians, elected Donald Trump.

But if allowed to be formed, the proposed new Italian government can start the long overdue process of saving Europe from ten years' stagnation after the crash triggered by London and Wall Street banks, and from blows to its productive industries by anti-Russia sanctions; and from another, worse financial crash which is looming over America and Europe.

The key will be establishing the Glass-Steagall Act, which both leading Italian parties want, to break up the big so-called "universal banks"—demanded by the European Union—that absorb trillions of bailout money from the European Central Bank and the U.S. Federal Reserve, and do not lend to anything productive. The second critical element: A national bank with the ability to issue credit for productive employment and new infrastructure, outside the EU austerity limits on government productive credit. Those two, if the parties can stick to them, can avert another financial blowout and start real economic growth again.

Both U.S. major parties put Glass-Steagall in their presidential platforms. President Trump called for it on the stump. Wall Street, however, has won out so far, and the megabanks have become even bigger, and more debt-leveraged, with bigger exposures to super-speculative derivatives contracts. As experts such as former FDIC officials Sheila Bair and Thomas Hoenig have been warning, that has made the financial system even more dangerous as interest rates rise on an unprecedented ocean of corporate debt, about to blow.

In Germany, the former chief economist of Europe's most dangerous huge bank, Deutsche Bank, gave an explosive interview on what ruined Deutsche Bank: "Anglo-American banking." A team of star speculators from Merrill Lynch in London and New York took over Germany's then-leading bank 20 years ago and turned it into a giant hedge fund that made huge profits every year—until it became clear the profits were faked and the bank was all but bankrupt.

Wall Street and London have won out so far, and the price has been economic stagnation with massive central bank money-printing, and another crash coming on. It Italy, there is a chance to start the reversal of that before it is too late.

EDITORIAL

In the United States, those Americans defending the presidency from a relentless coup attempt against President Donald Trump, have learned the hard way that London—British intelligence—started it, and is running it. Trump supporters are realizing you can't defend the presidency without attacking the British and London's anti-Russia, anti-China geopolitics.

That realization has even reached Congress, in the statements of Sen. Rand Paul. To quote one author's May 21 attack on the anti-Trump spying, "The British . . . have never hesitated to interfere in our domestic politics. . . . It happened in the run-up to both world wars, and it is happening today. If we trace the origins of the Russiagate hoax, and the campaign to dethrone Donald J. Trump, all roads lead to London."

The perpetrators of this hoax, even exposed, will not give it up; they have to be defeated. The British financial empire—the City of London that still dominates trans-Atlantic financial activity—also has to be defeated. Lyndon LaRouche underscored that necessity in his four economic laws that start with a Glass-Steagall bank breakup and "a return to a system of top-down, and thoroughly defined, National Banking" to unleash new technologies in new infrastructure, space exploration and science drivers to transform the economy.

In the face of another crash worse than 2008, Italy can be the start in saving Europe. Its leading parties are proposing what Americans wanted when they elected Donald Trump President. The challenge is the same: Defeat the City of London.

EIR Contents

www.larouchepub.com   Volume 45, Number 21, May 25, 2018

Cover This Week

Stefan Halper

LONDON IS EXPOSED AND VULNERABLE

THE THIRD OF LAROUCHE'S FOUR LAWS

Increasing Productivity and Potential Relative Population-Density

by Bill Roberts

May 21—It is up to those of us who are capable of doing so, to organize the base of support for launching an economic revolution within the United States. On the one hand, large swaths of the American population have come to distrust the leadership of both political parties, especially because of their incestuous relationship with Wall Street, and the domination of those parties by pro-war fanatics.

At the same time, however, if President Trump is going to move the country away from the control of the London and Wall Street monetary interests, he must have a knowledgeable base of supporters to do so. To mistrust and reject the seemingly powerful financial interests that have been running U.S. policy is one thing. To understand the rudiments of an economic science not predicated upon a belief in the intrinsic value of money, is an entirely different attribute, one found less frequently among the American electorate.

The third of the three pledges of the LaRouche PAC 2018 Campaign to Win the Future is the following: "I will implement LaRouche's Four Laws for Economic Recovery."

Although LaRouche's Four Laws represent a top-down programmatic blueprint for economic recovery and cannot be taken as separate policies, each of those four laws requires the reader to dive deeply into the implications of these measures. Probably the best starting point for acquiring such an in-depth understanding, is the voluminous writings of the author of the proposal,

cc/Tim Evanson

First U.S. Secretary of the Treasury Alexander Hamilton established 'The First National Bank of the United States' in 1791, chartered by the U.S. Congress, to improve the nation's credit.

Lyndon LaRouche. In particular *So You Wish to Learn All About Economics* and a video presentation produced to accompany that text, *The Power of Labor,* are both excellent places to begin.

In particular, let's dive into the third of the LaRouche Four Laws prescription. Laws one and two call for the reinstatement of the Glass-Steagall Act and the creation of a National Bank to issue credit for economic development. Glass-Steagall enjoys broad popular support. President Trump campaigned on it, and it is part of both the Democratic and Republican Party platforms, although there is presently no serious effort among the majority of either party to reinstate the law, as it is obvious that such an effort will represent an all-out crusade against the City of London and Wall Street. Not depending upon private sources of money for economic development, but rather returning to "a system of top-down, and thoroughly defined, National Banking," is less popular as a policy. It has its supporters, even if many of those supporters really wouldn't have a clue how to organize credit properly. Which brings us to LaRouche's Third Law:

> The purpose of the use of a Federal Credit System, is to generate high productivity trends in improvements of employment, with the accompanying intention, to increase the standard of living of the persons and households of the United States.

Speaker of the U.S. House of Representatives Paul Ryan.

U.S. Senator Bernie Sanders.

What do you suppose would be the most common objections to using the power of the federal government to issue credit for infrastructure and for various capital investments in industry, for the purpose of generating "high productivity trends in improvements of employment"?

Speaker of the House Paul Ryan wouldn't want the Federal government to spend any money on infrastructure if he could avoid it. Senator Bernie Sanders and progressive Democrats want to raise the minimum wage to $15 per hour, but they couldn't care less how those people are employed, or even what proportion of our workforce is actually engaged in productive work. There is no base of support in any faction of any political party in Washington, D.C., for investing credit in such a way as to make possible increased employment in manufacturing, or increasing the productivity of the workforce associated with the agro-industrial economy. The most meaningful expression of support for such a policy by any elected official is President Donald Trump's call for returning to the "American System" of Alexander Hamilton to build large-scale infrastructure and build up manufacturing.

Looking at those who object to credit allocations being directed to the necessity of building up the productivity of our workforce; let us ask the question: What is their underlying belief structure that leads to this objection?

Whether any individual objector is aware of his or her underlying beliefs or not, what shapes such thinking about economic policymaking is an implicit belief in the idea that mankind exists in a fixed relation to nature, a zero-growth state, a state of equilibrium. Either mankind does not actually create any really new economic potential without drawing down or destroying some other aspect of our productive potential (as the radical environmentalists tend to believe), or else the means by which governments are able to organize such trends in overall economic growth are not knowable to mankind in a hard and fast scientific way, as the free market libertarians believe.

In sum: He or she believes that man is nothing other than another animal species. Any improvement in the standard of living of one group of people, in some way has a corresponding negative effect on other populations or on man's relationship to "nature."

Anti-Entropy vs. British Economics

Lyndon LaRouche's economic ideas start from no such assumption, but rather proceed from a fundamentally different question: How does society reproduce itself at a higher level? Each generation produces the means of existence of the next generation by doing something new, by doing something better, by planning out the future. Perhaps it has been the lack of commitment to *this* that is responsible for the impoverished, drug-addicted state of our people. Perhaps the horrible conditions our people are living in, are not simply a result of a lot of bad individual choices.

Let's look at why, in his economics, Lyndon LaRouche emphasizes that this is the fundamental question. What determines the long-term successful survival of society? What is the metric of the fitness for survival of a nation? It is certainly *not* any sort of monetary measurement. There is obviously a tremendous amount of fakery involved in Wall Street and related monetary-profit measurements.

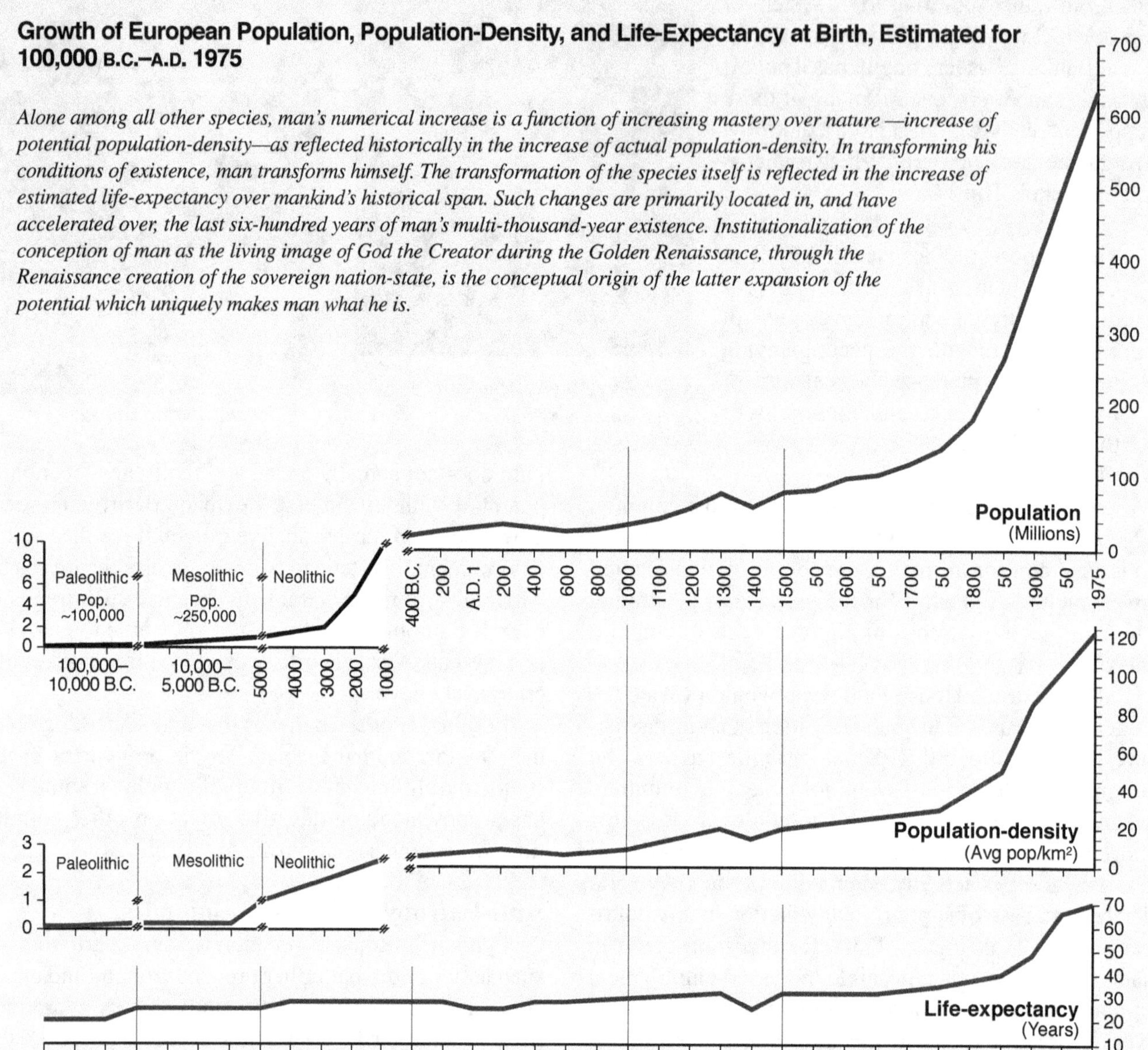

All charts are based on standard estimates compiled by existing schools of demography. None claim any more precision than the indicative; however, the scaling flattens out what might otherwise be locally, or even temporally, significant variation, reducing all thereby to the set of changes which is significant, independant of the quality of estimates and scaling of the graphs. Sources: For population and population-density, Colin McEvedy and Richard Jones, *Atlas of World Population History*; for life-expectancy, various studies in historical demography.

Note breaks and changes in scales.

According to LaRouche, the measure for the economic progress of a society is what he calls Potential Relative Population-Density.

We now exist at population potentials more than 400 times greater than what can be sustained by the most basic, hunting-and-gathering society. If we consider how many individuals of a particular species can be sustained on an average square mile of land, there is no animal species physiologically comparable to man

that has ever undergone such an upward transformation in average population density. The population characteristics of man since the European Renaissance, but even more dramatically since the development of chemistry as a modern science in the 1700s, have allowed the human population on this planet to increase at a hyperbolic rate.

One of the greatest leaps, if not the greatest leap, in mankind's ability to support increased numbers of people, is the mass production of chemical fertilizers. With chemical fertilizer, the productive capacity of agricultural land is not limited to the characteristics of the land as mankind finds it, but man is able to chemically design what is necessary to generate the greatest crop yield possible.

The introduction of heat-powered machinery into industry in the 1700s enabled a shift away from animal and human labor to *artificial labor*. Now one person operating a machine could accomplish, at a lower energy cost per unit of product, the labor of many men.

Let's look at a very basic example of how this works: The difference between subsistence agriculture, as against agriculture within an advanced industrial economy. That is, let's look at the difference between farming using only animal and human labor with no added chemical fertilizer, as compared to farming with mechanized tillage, planting, cultivation, chemical fertilizer, and irrigation if necessary.

The first thing we notice is that the nature of the energy consumed shifts from human and animal labor, to energy used to produce fertilizer and run mechanized equipment. The second thing that is apparent, is that the total energy applied per unit of land area increases slightly. However, the crop yields per unit of land area increase to a greater degree than the energy consumed per unit area. What this means is that while food produced per land area increases substantially, the total energy consumed per ton of food is lowered significantly.

Considering the effect of such a transformation on society generally, the following occurs: (1) given the increased productivity of any given farm, less of the population will be required to produce the food requirements of society, and (2) more people are going to be able to live off of the same amount of land.

This is perhaps the most basic example of how technological progress, leading to increases in the productive

Multi-row corn harvester in Ohio, Oct. 17, 2017.

powers of labor, is directly measurable in terms of how many people potentially can exist for any given square mile of land.

Population Control: The Death of Mankind

Consider something further: What happens when we limit changes to the current level of technology? At any fixed level of technology, as time goes on, that

Computer-controlled spot welding in a BMW plant in Leipzig, Germany, using industrial robots manufactured in Germany by KUKA (Keller und Knappich Augsburg).

economy's set of resources (petroleum, sources of chemical fertilizers) will be drawn down and depleted. The amount of energy, or cost to society, required to acquire the same resources, just to maintain current levels of production, will necessarily increase as that draw-down occurs. In other words, at any fixed technological level, the economic potential of society will wind down. There is no such thing as a society existing in a fixed relationship with nature. A zero-growth society is not possible. Without endless technological progress, society is doomed.

In his 1984 video presentation, *The Power of Labor*, LaRouche describes why our standard for measuring economic progress is not merely potential relative population-density, but rather the rate of increase in potential relative population-density:

> One of the unavoidable byproducts of technological progress is that the division of labor in production becomes increasingly complex. As a result, the size of the population must be increased. This means that the precondition for the survival of society is an endless increase in the potential relative population-density.

What this means for us today, is that it is both possible and necessary to increase the standard of living of our workforce, increase the productivity and profit of our economy overall, and increase the size of our population. While this conception of progress, what we might call the "general welfare principle," was referred to by American System economists from Alexander Hamilton onward, Lyndon LaRouche's work on the anti-entropic nature of human economy is the strongest refutation of British economics, with its zero-growth axiomatics.

Embedded in the American Mind

America's founding fathers were quite aware that such a process of continual growth and advancement only happens in a society which fosters individual human creativity. The United States was born out of a

Reconstructed forge with bellows of the Saugus Iron Works, dating from the 1600s in the colonial era in Massachusetts.

conscious project to create an educated society, a society free of the disease of oligarchism, capable of reproducing itself. Long before the American Revolution, as far back as the early days of the Massachusetts Bay Colony in 1645, the colonies in North America were developing iron furnaces and mills, to have the ability to develop labor-saving tools of all types, including for agriculture. In fact, by 1776, the newly independent United States was the third-largest producer of iron in the world, after only Sweden and Russia.

A critical issue hampering the self-advancement of the American colonies was population control. One of the chief causes of gdependence against the British Crown, was that gain.

Support for the necessity for the Federal Government to issue credit for the promotion of high productivity trends in employment within the economy, should be considered a basic indication of competence for candidates running for City Council or County Commissioner, let alone the U.S. Congress.

The continued survival of the United States, necessarily in peaceful cooperation with the other major-power nations, requires a new political configuration capable of expressing this quality of productive American identity, informed by Lyndon LaRouche's identification of the secret, actual source of economic value.

The Mass Strike ... or, Grasping the Shelley Moment

by Robert Ingraham

May 18—What is the true potential of the present moment? What is it that is not only desirable, but is now possible, to accomplish?

Many people, within our culture, are trapped behind the blinders of pessimism, seeing no way out of the omnipresent seeming reality of poverty, drug addiction, war, and cultural hedonism. Others—including many among those who voted for Donald Trump—sense that we are now living in a period of great opportunity, even a potential for a transformative change in the direction of our society. In many ways this potential is not palpable, but its existence as a cultural force is undeniable. Yes, in the trans-Atlantic world, we all exist within a deeply pessimistic oligarchical culture, but to jump to the conclusion that the overwhelming majority of citizens are personally pessimistic would be a grave error. The continued support for President Trump, despite an almost uniform hostility from the major media and political parties, is itself a "proof of principle" that many, many Americans yearn for positive change.

It also must be recognized, although the full implications of this will not be discussed here, that America is not an island. Since at least 2015, we have witnessed many manifestations of hopeful political upsurge throughout the world, and this process has been greatly aided by the optimism engendered by the China-led Belt and Road Initiative. This is a global phenomenon. Old policy axioms are being discarded, and everywhere governments and leaders are looking for "a new way to do things."

Some politically astute observers have described the turbulence of the current environment as a "Mass Strike" period. But what precisely is the nature of this Mass Strike? And what does this imply as to the actual nature of the opportunity which exists, as well as the responsibility this places on each of us? History presents opportunities, but those opportunities exist only as potentialities. They must be acted upon; yet, all action is not equal. The difference between victory and defeat rests on understanding the nature of the intervention which is required. This is where the issue of leadership arises.

The implication of this is that a great personal challenge is presented to the individual who desires to play a part in effecting positive political change.

The Future Potential

The term Mass Strike is usually associated with the history of Marxism, and most of the commentary and analysis of the term is sloppy drivel. Of all of the Marxist theorists, it was Rosa Luxemburg who presented the most rigorous definition of the term, particularly in her differentiation of the strategic nature of the Mass Strike from the tactical initiative of the General Strike. Luxemburg's intellectual courage is praiseworthy, and her insights into the political crisis of her own time stand head-and-shoulders above her contemporaries. We need, however, to broaden our investigation, and examine current potentials through the lens of Lyndon LaRouche's understanding of human history.

We will begin with a negative. Most people have a populist "from the bottom up" notion of humanity's

CC/James McNellis

Trump supporters at the 2017 presidential inauguration.

struggle for a better future. In such a view, a Mass Strike—or any other type of revolutionary upsurge—is seen as a Resistance to Tyranny. You have a people who are being oppressed, who are being ground into the dirt under the Iron Heel (to use Jack London's phrase) of a ruling class or institution—a people who "rise up" against their suffering and oppression.

This scenario is most certainly *not* a Mass Strike. It better describes incidents such as the 1943 Warsaw Ghetto Uprising. Under conditions where a people are facing extinction, or where they are driven beyond the limits of endurance, resistance may be their only option, and the participants may be both heroic and noble. Yet, this is not where great historical change originates.

Great change in a time of crisis, great breakthroughs in the human condition, are always born of optimism. And they always occur under conditions where a growing number of people open their minds to the implications of revolutionary advances in science, economics, and art, as those discoveries are developed by the leaders of their time. People begin to glimpse— even if only as an itch in the back of their minds—the possibility of a better future, a future framed in new principles, superior to the axioms and beliefs which have kept them in chains. That potential future, and those new principles, will provide inspiration. They define the "spirit of the age," but to succeed, the "spirit must become flesh," and to accomplish that requires a leadership willing to undergo the most ruthless self-examination of their own beliefs as to the nature of the human species. Most important, they must be willing to become actors on the stage, to take personal responsibility to lead the fight for a better future.

Intense and Impassioned Conceptions

Let us view the concept of Mass Strike from a different perspective. In 1821, Percy Shelley authored *A Defence of Poetry*. A concluding portion of that essay —one which is very well known and often quoted—is directly relevant to the subject under discussion. That passage bears repeating here:

> At such periods there is an accumulation of the power of communicating and receiving intense and impassioned conceptions respecting man and nature. The persons in whom this power resides may often, as far as regards many portions of their nature, have little apparent correspondence with that spirit of good of which they are the ministers.
>
> But even whilst they deny and abjure, they are yet compelled to serve, the power which is seated on the throne of their own soul. It is impossible to read the compositions of the most celebrated writers of the present day without being startled with the electric life which burns within their words. They measure the circumference and sound the depths of human nature with a comprehensive and all-penetrating spirit, and they are themselves perhaps the most sincerely astonished at its manifestations; for it is less their spirit than the spirit of the age.

Percy B. Shelley

What Shelley is describing is the quality of optimism and hope which defines all moments of great potential change. Optimism, properly nurtured, creates miracles. However, what is necessary is to understand from whence such optimism arises, and to answer the question, how might it be brought to bloom?

Think of Uncle Remus, walking down the country lane, whistling a tune, happy in his servitude. This is the Walt Disney version of optimism. That is clearly not what is required. Think also of the momentary pleasures derived by immersion in the culture of drug usage. This is the opposite of optimism, the fleeting attempt to escape from a life for which no positive future might be perceived.

What we require to appreciate Shelley's words is something far more rigorous. In that regard, let Johannes Kepler and Lyndon LaRouche be our guides.

What we find in both men is an unshakable morality as to a dedication of their lives toward improving mankind's future, combined with a courageous determination to strive for demonstrable scientific truth—to unmask the secrets of the lawful universe. It is in the personalities of Kepler and LaRouche that the secret of the Mass Strike is revealed.

Courage and Genius

To become an effective leader in a revolutionary situation, it is necessary to abandon almost all of what you thought was true about human social reproduction. The most ruthless examination of one's "knowledge" of economics, science, music, and history is required. A willingness to

Dante Alighieri

change is a prerequisite.

Contrary to what is asserted in the multitude of nonsensical history books, all great moments of change in human history have been made possible by profound breakthroughs in Mankind's understanding of the nature of the universe and the nature of the human identity. Those breakthroughs, and the personal courage exhibited to accomplish them, were the catalysts that made possible the visualization of a more productive future. They were the indispensable keys in the emergence of a new Spirit, as Shelley discusses it.

Let us take a few examples to reference the point at hand:

Think of Dante Alighieri and Giotto di Bondone. It was Dante's Promethean development of the Italian

'Benjamin Franklin Drawing Electricity from the Sky.'

vernacular which unleashed powerful, hitherto unrealized, cognitive potentials within the Italian population. It was Dante's—and his ally Giotto's—examination of the nature of the human mind which shattered the straightjacket of a feudalist culture. Centuries later, the publication of Alessandro Manzoni's *I Promessi Sposi* (*The Betrothed*) and the 1841 premiere of Giuseppe Verdi's opera *Nabucco* would play a similar role in sparking the cultural upsurge leading into the Italian Risorgimento.

Take the case also of the American Revolution. It was the *scientist* Benjamin Franklin who was the true author of the American Republic, an intention which he made clear as early as 1733, when in

J.S. Bach

Poor Richard's Almanac he assigns the date of birth of Richard Saunders (the pseudonym chosen by Franklin to be the publisher of the almanac) as October 23, 1684, the precise day that the British throne had abolished the Charter of the Massachusetts Bay colony. In Philadelphia, Franklin established the Junto in 1727 and the American Philosophical Society in 1744. More to the point, Franklin, together with his collaborator Cadwallader Colden, became the key allies of the pro-Leibniz German scientific circles led by Abraham Kästner and Rudolph Erich Raspe.[1] As early as 1741, Franklin had

---

1. Shavin, David, "Leibniz to Franklin On 'Happiness,'" *Fidelio*, Vol. 12, No. 1, Spring 2003.

obtained a copy of the *Leibniz-Clarke Correspondence* for his Library Company of Philadelphia, and in 1766 he spent ten days in Germany with Raspe and visited Kästner at Göttingen University, where Franklin's experiments in electricity—and the implications of those experiments as to the nature of the physical universe—were discussed. It was the 1765 Raspe/Kästner publication of Leibniz' *New Essays on Human Understanding*—and Leibniz' devastating critique of John Locke—which would provide the moral and philosophical basis for the Declaration of Independence.

Even earlier, we find the intervention of Johann Sebastian Bach, with the 1722 issuance of his *Das Wohltempierte Klavier* (*The Well-Tempered Clavier*), a work greatly influenced by the studies and proposi-

Revolution of Abraham Lincoln.

Many other examples could be given—such as the movement led by Martin Luther King—but the point to be made is the role of the individual leader in uplifting and fighting the battle at the highest cultural and philosophical level—never pandering to the tactics and "practical" outlook that are commonplace among opportunistic politicians and others.

Lyndon LaRouche's Challenge

In the years following World War II, Lyndon LaRouche created a revolution in economics—in the scientific understanding of the social reproduction of the human species. Of particular importance for our present discussion were LaRouche's refutation of Informa-

Lyndon H. LaRouche, Jr. (center) at the founding meeting of the Fusion Energy Foundation, with Dr. Louis Gold, leading nuclear scientist and member of the FEF Scientific Advisory Committee (left) and Mr. Rice, a representative of the Atomic Energy Commission (right).

EIRNS

tion Theory and his application of Bernhard Riemann's non-Euclidian approach to the nature of the physical universe. From those studies, LaRouche was able to take the original economic works of Leibniz and Alexander Hamilton and develop them even further.

tions of both Johannes Kepler and Gottfried Leibniz. Bach unveils an entirely new language—one of well-tempered polyphony—and he demonstrates that this language is coherent with both the human mind and the principles which underlie the nature of the universe. An entirely new cognitive power is unleashed.

Later we see the repercussions of Friedrich Schiller's devastating repudiation of Immanuel Kant's concept of the human identity. Not only did German patriots go into battle with copies of Schiller's poems in their breast pockets during the 1813-1814 War of Liberation, but Schiller's ideas would cross the Atlantic and reverberate, contributing to the Second American

LaRouche's approach has always proceeded from the standpoint of "Man, the creator"—i.e., the singular reality that the human mind partakes and contributes in the continuing process of universal creation. It was LaRouche who developed the concept of Potential Relative Population Density as a physical economic marker to define a "measurement" as to the success or failure of economic and scientific policy, and it was LaRouche who defined the potential for a non-entropic development of the human species.[2]

Between 1974 and 1976, Lyndon LaRouche created the Fusion Energy Foundation; he authored his proposal for "The International Development Bank"; his textbook *Dialectical Economics*—which had already circulated for a number of years in manuscript form—was published; and he launched his 1976 campaign for the Presidency.

In the 1980s and 1990s LaRouche's writings were studied intensively throughout the world, including among some of the highest leadership circles in Russia, China, and India. The effects of that intervention are witnessed today, including in the China-led Belt and Road Initiative. LaRouche never pandered.

General Douglas MacArthur (center) at Inchon, Korea, 1950.

He never prostituted himself. He never compromised on principle. His challenge was always "Come up to my level!"

Hard Work

Many people who are involved in politics complain about the population. The refrain usually goes, "We could accomplish such great things, if only the population weren't so backward." Such analyses are the hallmarks of moral failures, of individuals who refuse to accept the true nature of their primary responsibility. To organize others, one must begin with organizing one's self. The problem is always with the leadership, never the population. The state of the population is simply part of the battleground. Every great military commander and political leader recognizes that.

Think in military terms. Think of Washington after his retreat across New Jersey, Grant confronted with the impregnable Vicksburg, or MacArthur just prior to the Inchon landing. Yes, they were faced with daunting battlefield conditions, and their individual military genius allowed them to accomplish glorious victories. Yet, an insightful military leader also understands that the "battleground" with which he must contend includes the minds and morale of his own troops and commanders.

Today, we have an objective political battle we are waging, both in the United States and world-wide. But, the key battleground is that being fought for the minds and hearts of the population. That is where the fight will ultimately be lost or won.

The proper role of individual leadership is to act as the midwife in giving birth to the new "Spirit of the Age," to awaken those potentials which lie dormant in the hearts of their fellow creatures. The leadership required must never be pedantic, but must strive for challenging the most firmly held axioms within those being addressed, and to awaken that spark of creativity which exists in every human being. However, to succeed, anyone involved in this type of work must begin with a commitment to his or her own self-perfection. There is a great joyfulness to be found in such work, but it is a joyfulness that is incompatible with self-satisfaction or mental laziness.

Each week *Executive Intelligence Review* publishes an article written by Lyndon LaRouche. If you are not reading these articles—fighting to master the concepts presented—then you will never be an effective political leader. You will operate on a much lower—and impotent—level. LaRouche built his own movement, his intended intelligentsia, as a leadership organization. If you want to change history, why would you settle for anything less?

____

2. For more on LaRouche's personal role and the development of his movement, see the edited transcript of Barbara Boyd's address to the May 12, 2018 Manhattan meeting, printed in this issue of *EIR*.

How Lyndon LaRouche Built a Political Organization from Scratch

by Barbara Boyd

EIRNS

Lyndon LaRouche in 1973.

May 19—LaRouche PAC, the political action committee founded in 2004 by Lyndon LaRouche, has launched a national campaign in the context of the 2018 midterm elections, to secure the future of the United States. That campaign centers on three pledges that any candidate for Congress must endorse before receiving endorsement by the PAC. LaRouche PAC is taking this campaign to as many Congressional Districts as possible, seeking out the constituency leaders in those districts whom Congressional candidates will have to recruit in order to win the vote in those November 2018 elections.

The Political Action Committee is targeting and building a movement of the economy's producers: skilled workers, farmers, scientists, engineers, manufacturers, builders, police, fire fighters, other first responders, doctors and nurses, teachers, trade unionists, and civil rights organization leaders. This new movement will insist that candidates pledge to work to stop the illegal and unconstitutional coup against President Trump, to secure U.S. participation in China's "One Belt, One Road" great development initiative for the world's economies, and to implement LaRouche's Four Laws for Economic Recovery of the United States.

This requires a great and uncompromising educational effort, designed to immerse volunteers to the campaign in the unique discoveries found in Lyndon LaRouche's science of political economy and the accompanying philosophical, historical, and scientific issues which flow from those discoveries. At the center of the campaign is the new pamphlet, "LaRouche's Four Laws for Economic Recovery—A New Paradigm for Mankind," just released by LaRouche PAC, elabo-

rating the three pledges and their necessity in the mission to rescue the citizens of the United States from the despair and economic devastation produced by the Wall Street/City of London monstrosity known as the "post-industrial society."

Fortunately, this campaign has a model to build from. That model is Lyndon LaRouche's original building of the National Caucus of Labor Committees, a political organization he built from scratch in the period 1968-1974, based on a series of classes featuring a thorough and devastating epistemological critique of Karl Marx and which successfully challenged class participants to assimilate and employ the philosophical conceptions of Plato, Kepler, Leibniz, Carl Friedrich Gauss, Bernhard Riemann and others in mobilizing their own mental powers and creativity to change the world.

On May 14, Barbara Boyd, LaRouche PAC's treasurer, spoke to the regular Manhattan Project meeting of LaRouche PAC about LaRouche PAC's 2018 campaign. We thought it important to bring this perspective _to EIR's readers. What follows is an edited transcript of that Manhattan event._

Boyd: The image I'd like you to think about to begin this presentation is what John F. Kennedy said before a large audience at Rice University on September 12, 1962. He said to that audience, and to the American people as a whole, "We choose to go to the Moon in this decade and do the other things, not because they are easy, but because they are hard, because that goal will serve to organize and measure the best of our energies and skills, because that challenge is one that we are willing to accept, one we are unwilling to postpone, and one which we intend to win." We were going to go to the Moon because it was a necessary thing we had to do as a population at that point in history. And he proceeded to lay out that grand vision.

Did he know at that particular point in time, when he laid out that mission, that the Moon mission was going to return ten-to-one in terms of advanced technological spin-offs resulting from that investment, which would increase the productivity of the population and the economy as a whole? Did he know that for a fact? Did he know each step in the process by which we would get to the Moon? In other words, did he have a map in front of him that said "Step A in my plan for going to Moon is the following, and it's to be funded at such and such a level"? Or rather, wasn't it that he had an idea of the direction in which he wanted to go, the direction in which it could be funded? And he set the country off on a mission which stimulated the creativity of the entire population, a mission with the stipulation and constraint of his insisting that we cannot fail in this mission. It is absolutely necessary. We have to do this. This is what has to happen at this point if this country is going to survive as a nation. We have to take a great journey to the Moon.

Think about that in contradistinction to today. If a President Trump, for example, stands up and says, "I want to go back to the Moon," the first thing that happens is, everybody says, "OK, where's your plan for the Moon? How much is it going to cost for each step? And where are we going to get the money from?" We seem to have lost the ability which President Kennedy had to deliver an open-ended invitation to the citizens of the United States to engage in a great journey, a great adventure, challenging fundamental conceptions about

President John F. Kennedy delivering his 1961 inaugural address.

man, nature, and how things work, in which everybody has a stake in a mission which seems almost impossible at the point you actually start to talk about it. I say that any creative and necessary mission involves a directed passion, the idea that _I have to do this and I cannot fail._ You really don't know how to break it down into those kinds of steps and details or anything else. You're simply challenged. You stay up at night, you burn the candles. You talk to people; you come up with ideas, you try them, you experiment. You figure out whether it works or doesn't work, or what happens. Think about that in terms of the small number of people who think like that today in our country after years of living in a de-industrialized economy.

The 2018 Elections and the Lessons of 2016

So, when you look at the 2018 midterms, it's very clear that in terms of the coup, its plan of attack is, "Let's round up a lot of politicians, be they Democrats or Republicans or independents. The only thing they have to do to be qualified is, they have to pledge, 'I'm going to impeach Donald Trump.' " Their plan is to go back to the type of imperial framework implicit in the Clinton and Obama campaign operations, and most certainly in the Bush administration—what we'll call the casino economy, the post-industrial society that has driven most of the United States into what was really a foreseeable degradation of the entire population.

Take out an electoral map of the results of the 2016 election. This is normally done in terms of red colors for where Trump was triumphant and blue colors for where Clinton won. What you see is almost the entirety of the spatial United States of America is red, except for the coasts.

When we began to look at this issue of what's going to happen in the 2018 elections, we asked ourselves, "OK, how do you actually put together a nationwide coalition which is not only going to stop the coup, but is actually going to be enforcing the promises Trump made in the election, the promises which caused all of those people to vote for him?" They didn't vote for him because of immigration, and they didn't vote for him because of racial dog whistles. His own campaign analysis of the so-called Rust Belt or Midwestern states, was that the real messages that resonated with people, that absolutely made them turn out to vote, were his promises to rebuild the infrastructure of the United States, to rebuild the United States economy; and to stop being the world's policeman, to stop intervening in the affairs of other nations all over the world. Those were the two promises that his own campaign data says won him the election. The coup has actually been a huge impediment to the very urgent discussion which we need to have with citizens to enforce the promises upon which he was elected.

Three Pledges

I am going to focus on one of the three pledges in LaRouche PAC's 2018 campaign platform. I think everyone in this room has had ample opportunity to understand what China is doing and what this New Paradigm is, in the world. What I want to concentrate on here is the United States of America, and what we do here today. Therefore, I really want to focus a lot more than anything else on what the pamphlet has to say about LaRouche's Four Laws for Economic Recovery.

When we wrote the new pamphlet, we were aware of various problems people have in thinking about this. People tend to say, "OK, let's go on a big campaign for Glass-Steagall, and maybe we can do something on that, and that'll work. OK?" The obverse is the thing which is currently going on at least as I hear it in various organizers' discussions of the Four Laws: "Well, really the most important thing is the Fourth Law. That's what we should really be focussing on." All of that is just fundamentally incorrect; it's an incorrect perception of what Lyndon LaRouche laid out in the Four Laws. It's a unitary conception there. All of it has to happen at

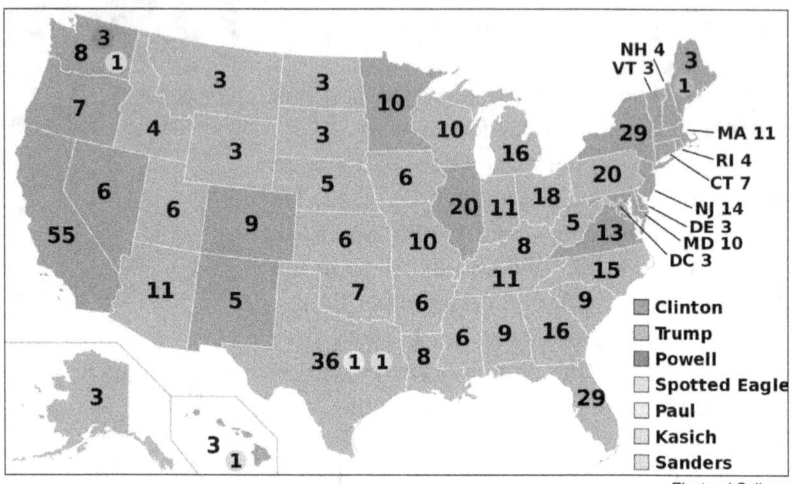

2016 Presidential election results map. Red denotes states won by Trump/Pence, blue denotes those won by Clinton/Kaine. Bold numbers indicate electoral votes allotted to the winner of each state.

once to actually achieve the type of economic breakthroughs he is presenting. I find particularly telling, in a lot of the discussions I have had, how much we skip over the third of the four laws. I will just read his formulation of it, to remind you of what it says:

> The purpose of the use of a Federal Credit-system, is to generate high-productivity trends in improvements of employment, with the accompanying intention, to increase the physical-economic productivity and the standard of living of the persons and households of the United States.

The reason why I emphasize that, is that you can portray the Fourth Law, the demand for a crash program to develop fusion power and its consequences for space exploration, as a kind of dreamy, wonderful concept. You can say, we'll get a fusion economy, or the Chinese will come in and build things, or we build big infrastructure, and everything will, as a result, automatically improve. That's not necessarily true if you are not employing the measurement which Lyndon LaRouche discovered and talked about over his entire career in economics, which is called "potential relative population density."

That is, how do you invest your funds once Glass-Steagall stops the hot-money flows, once a national bank or similar mechanism concentrates credit? The constraints he applies in the third law, govern what kind of investment you must make: Investments that increase potential relative population density, which follows in the wake of high productivity trends in employment, increases in physical economic productivity, and increases in the standard of living of persons and households—the capacity for a society to actually reproduce itself at a higher level of productivity than that which existed before. That's what the Third Law imposes as a constraint on how you're investing your money. It involves "soft infrastructure" such as healthcare and education. It's not just railroads, it's not just high-speed trains. It's what's going on in a population; what's going on in education; what's going on with culture, which results in the fostering of creative individuals. What are the constraints you have to create within the living standards of the population of the United States, so that you can self-consciously create people who are going to be creative? The Fourth Law, the crash program to develop fusion, allows you to create a whole new economic platform based on a transformative energy source, guaranteeing that you can sustain the economic productivity and standards of living of the Third Law far into the future.

A Unitary Concept

So, the idea here, once we get that correction into it, is that the Four Laws present a unitary concept which has to be grasped as such by the individual citizen. How do we create an educational campaign which can ensure that that happens?

Some of you have been around us for a long, long time; some of you have been around us for a very short period of time. But I went way, way back when I was thinking about this in terms of our present situation as an organization in the United States, and what's actually going on with the population which we saw manifested in the vote for Trump in the 2016 election. I looked at the phenomenon of the pivot counties in the electoral map. That is, those places where they voted for Obama in 2008, they voted for Obama in 2012; but they voted for Trump in 2016. No matter how much else you might sociologically characterize it—and these people have been interviewed as if they are archaeological specimens of some type by innumerable

reporters—essentially, they voted for change.

They said, "My life sucks at this point. I'm ready to do anything to change this. I don't care if you say that Donald Trump shot 40 people on Wall Street. If he's going to shake up this horrible situation I'm in, I'm for him. I want change." And they still want change! Their whole world has been completely shaken up.

People were not simply responding to the slogan "Make America Great Again" as a simple form of nostalgia for the 1950s and 1960s, when there was some social stability, steady jobs, and the ability to buy a house and raise a family. Greatness requires a great leader, like Kennedy, inviting the American people's participation in a large and great mission like the Space Program. Most people, then, embraced it, most having gone through World War II, another great national endeavor in which the result was not obvious from the beginning. But those positive developments did not prevent the catastrophe we have lived through subsequently. Our program, the LaRouche Program, has to be to "Make America great, in a self-sustaining way, so that we don't repeat the nonsense that we've gone through over the past 20 years."

Intellectual Toughness: A Producer's Coalition

So, I went back and read—and I recommend that people willing to lead, re-read—a little piece which Lyndon LaRouche published in *The Campaigner* magazine of October 1974, a piece titled, "The Conceptual History of the National Caucus of Labor Committees." In Section III of that piece, "How to Start a New Movement," LaRouche discusses how to build a socialist organization (or a political organization, I would say it today) from scratch. I will refer to certain excerpts, because it reflects exactly the idea that I had in thinking about what we call in the pamphlet "the producers' coalition." That is, that the people who voted for Trump and are most prone to become what we used to call "worker intellectuals," the leaders or the constituency leaders of whole sections of society—are more or less exactly what the Trump voter in the Midwest, for example, actually is.

The people who work in production, or who are responsible for running a business which produces a certain type of product, if they're more astute and they're in areas such as machine tools and other places, they are also fairly astute in terms of international relations. They understand what has to happen with their product in terms of selling it in the world at this point. Farmers understand a lot about economics already, because they've have to run an agricultural enterprise. They have to understand all sorts of things about how to invest in certain seed cycles; they have to understand a whole lot about fundamental science in order to run that farm.

In that piece, LaRouche says, Think of it this way: You have people who we'll call "trained professional organizers." Those are the people who are full-time in the developing organization. In order to qualify to be that professional organizer, you have to qualify yourself deeply in my economics. At that time, by that, he meant literally taking his Dialectical Economics (DE) course, which was, if people go back and actually are interested, and think about it in terms of today, when we're meeting with the Chinese, or we're interacting with the Russians, or we're interacting with those who call themselves socialists, DE is the best possible epistemological organizing vehicle, because it's a critique of Marxism from inside Marx, and inside a conception which we will call LaRouche's conception of the American System. Which is a fundamental advance, by the way, on the work of Alexander Hamilton.

It goes back to the emphasis I'm placing on the Third Law and Fourth Law. In fact, a group of Russian scientists and economists said that Lyndon LaRouche's fundamental discovery was discovering this measurement called "potential relative population density." In fact, they have a name for it in Russia; it's called the "La" for LaRouche. When we skip over the Third Law, we're missing the "LaRouche." In Lyndon LaRouche's 1987 article about this in the *EIR* magazine, "In Defense of Treasury Secretary Alexander Hamilton," he

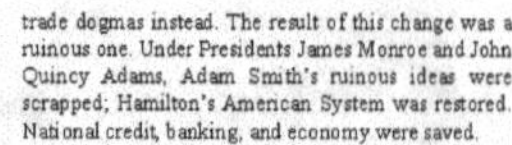

In Defense of Treasury Secretary Alexander Hamilton

by Lyndon H. LaRouche, Jr.

Note: Lyndon LaRouche was running for the Democratic Presidential nomination in 1987 at the time he wrote this paper. A version of this paper was issued by the LaRouche Democratic Campaign, and another as follows, was published in the July 3, 1987 EIR.

June 22, 1987—Today, Alexander Hamilton, our republic's first Treasury Secretary and Inspector General of our armed forces, seems to be a giant, and our contemporary political leaders Lilliputians by comparison.

When Hamilton entered the post of Treasury Secretary, our nation's indebtedness and economy were in a terrible condition, similar in many ways to the economic disaster we are suffering today. Under Hamilton's program of recovery, our national credit was restored, our banking system became the soundest in the world, and prosperous growth was unleashed throughout most of our nation.

These policies of credit, banking, and economy, which Hamilton outlined in his famous reports to the Congress, became admired and envied worldwide by the name of the "American System of political-economy."

Under the administrations of Thomas Jefferson and James Madison, Treasury Secretary Gallatin scrapped the American System, and introduced Adam Smith's free-trade dogmas instead. The result of this change was a ruinous one. Under Presidents James Monroe and John Quincy Adams, Adam Smith's ruinous ideas were scrapped; Hamilton's American System was restored. National credit, banking, and economy were saved.

Presidents Jackson and van Buren destroyed the American System, and reintroduced the ruinous policies of Adam Smith. The result of Jackson's policies was the terrible Panic of 1837.

I have lived personally through a similar experience in my own lifetime. The Coolidge and Hoover use of Adam Smith's policies, during the 1920s, plunged the world into a Great Depression. Most Americans suffered greatly through 1938, until President Franklin

A parade in New York City celebrates the ratification of the U.S. Constitution in July, 1788, with a parade featuring the ship Hamilton, named for the chief author of The Federalist papers. Under Hamilton's "American System" of economics, the United States entered an era of prosperous growth.

says, "Were Alexander Hamilton alive today, he would smile as he accused me of 'stealing his program.' Then Hamilton would ask, 'Show me how you worked out the methods for measuring the connection between rates of technological progress and rates of increase of productive powers of labor.' We wouldn't talk about much else, since on everything else we would agree automatically."

LaRouche Takes Hamilton to New Heights

So Lyndon LaRouche fundamentally advances Hamilton, and that's really implicit in the Third and Fourth Laws. When reading the Four Laws, the way people have tended to look at it, is, "Well, he's got this whole piece at the end of the Four Laws as he wrote them, about the nature of man, and the nature of mind. That's really all a part of the Fourth Law." I would say, "No, it's not." The last piece is typical of Lyndon LaRouche's writing, which is like Beethoven or someone else who writes a wonderful musical composition, and in fact, that last piece is really a principled recapitulation of why he wrote everything he did in all Four Laws. And the Four Laws themselves are a unitary concept.

Again, you can't do one without doing them all, if we're going to take the United States to the economic level we need at this point, to actually be a leading force in the world again for the good.

When LaRouche speaks about the type of educational class required to qualify someone to be a professional organizer, it is a little bit different than the way we talk about education today. He wrote, "The first and most obvious purpose is to begin turning potential recruits into qualified professional organizers. The second purpose is to present the class material on a sufficiently high level of quality as to drive away a majority of radicalized university students."

So, what is he talking about? We say, we want to recruit people to us based on some "agreement." He says, no, I'm going to design a class which is of sufficiently high level to drive all but the most serious people away. Not only that, the level of the class and the strug-

Labor Committee member Alan Ogden organizing at a plant gate in Virginia, 1977.

than the previous generation by this amount. Hopefully, I started a new renaissance, and I set the template for you, and the new generation will respond in turn. It's my responsibility, therefore, not to go off and smoke dope, not to sit in a room and look at social media, not to do this and do that. It's my responsibility to do exactly what I just said for the next generation that comes after me.

Passion To Build an Organization and Be an Organizer

So, the idea Lyndon LaRouche presented, as to how to build an organization, was twofold. One is to set up an organizing process in which we are capable of having classes and rapidly identifying those people who fit into the realm of, "I've got this passion; I want to do it, I want to be a professional organizer in the Labor Committee." The second is to broadly give the program to those sectors of the population that can actually rapidly assimilate that program and help us turn it into reality. That's the whole secret sauce here, and I stole it entirely from Lyndon LaRouche's paper called, "The Conceptual History of the Labor Committee," particularly his writings there on how to create a political organization from scratch.

In conceptualizing the new pamphlet, we went back to Lyndon LaRouche's 90th birthday speech to set the fundamental tone and agenda. In that speech, he said the political parties are both completely corrupt. They will be gotten rid of, because they are corrupt. They have no new ideas; they have no direction for the country; they have no place they're taking people to; they have no imagination. They're completely dominated by Wall Street, and their basic model of an economy is a British imperial model. But when the parties are destroyed, as they were in the 2016 election, the real power has been placed in the hands of the individual citizen, the republican citizen envisioned in the U.S. Constitution. How do you educate that individual citizen to take responsibility, and do so rapidly?

The most rapid way by which people get educated about fundamental concepts is when they have to teach them, when they have to go out and present them to somebody else. When they have to go out and stick

gle people have with it is going to change the person, so that they can stand on their own two feet and think originally, creatively. For those people that professional organizers go out to organize, are in the productive and skilled sectors of the population.

He says, "Look, these guys are living their everyday lives. They have jobs, they have families, and they have all of these other things tugging on them." It's the job of the professional organizer to develop the successful program for intervening in society so that those who are best situated to understand and act on it can do so.

Those in productive layers of society have an inherent understanding of what we're talking about when we talk about economics. If they're running a plant, they know what a process sheet is, they know what a bill of materials is, and they know what a bill of consumption is. They know about input/output tables in terms of what they're putting in and what they're getting out. What they don't understand, is what the professional organizer then gives them. In this case, it's the Third and Fourth Laws. We take the producers' knowledge of the plant and how it is run and we build on it the notion of how to build a platform for the entire economy which will last at least two generations into the future.

The professional organizers can prove to those he or she is organizing exactly why the Four Laws program is, as LaRouche specifies, not an option currently, but an urgent necessity. He or she can inspire, as Kennedy did, the great mission orientation in this population to bring this program into being. We will restore to this population the fundamental notion of social progress, where we can say to the next generation, I did better their foot in that water, and go meet with the mayor and say, "Look, I want you to back this program, and here's why." You have to prove it to him; you have to get it across. Sometimes, you'll go and stick your foot in the water, and you realize that you really didn't have it, and you screwed up and you didn't do it right.

But then you go back. Just like in any educational experience, you say to yourself, "OK, what did I do wrong? How did I present this wrong? How do I actually do it better?" And you go back. In this way, very quickly, you assimilate the fundamental concepts. Whereas, if you're sitting on the sidelines, and you're not doing stuff with us, and you're not part of actually going out and doing this organizing, what happens is, you're very disconnected from some very profound concepts which you have to get in your head—concepts you have to play with, you have to exploit, you have to teach with, to actually really begin to understand.

Defeating Hopelessness and Despair

The other thing I'll reference for just a second, because I can't get a certain book out of my head. This week I read *Dreamland* by Sam Quinones, which is mentioned in the Four Laws pamphlet. If you haven't read it, or haven't read Paul Gallagher's review of it in the May 11, 2018 *EIR*, titled "How a Nation Is Destroyed, and How It Can Save Itself," I think it's very important to do so. It shows us an essential obstacle to what it is we're talking about here that can only be overcome if we implement LaRouche's Four Laws. Sam Quinones discusses how the opioid epidemic has spread in the United States to the extent that, between that and the counterculture and everything we've been attacking for years, we're about to lose an entire generation or two.

For example, a figure that was given to me last week: 85% of young people in and around Buffalo, New York who apply for any job up there have a drug problem. When you look at the labor force that you're trying to bring into the idea of a crash fusion program, and you must say to yourself, wait a second, where's our labor force? That's who we're supposed to be talking to here, that's who is going to do all of this. We've

got a really, really big problem.

Quinones parallels what we've been saying in many respects. His work is known within the Trump administration. Attorney General Jeff Sessions has read *Dreamland*. In paragraph one of Gallagher's review, he quotes from a May 1 interview of Sessions by the *Washington Post*. Sessions asked his interviewer: "Have you read *Dreamland*? For the first time, you get a glimpse of how it [the American opioid addiction epidemic] really developed." Quinones tells how this happened. Well, he does and he doesn't. He tells you certain things about how it happened, which is very remarkable and a very good journalistic feat. He gives you the mechanisms by which the crisis was spread by the drug companies basically hooking people on pills; he exposes a very systematic brainwashing operation of the entirety of society, assisted by doctors who essentially prescribe many more pills than any population could possibly consume.

Then he describes how a retail drug operation in one state in Mexico, out of one small town, actually came in following the trail of the opioid epidemic and hooked people on a very strong form of heroin, which was sold and delivered almost like pizzas are. People could just dial up when they wanted a delivery. The whole idea was, first get the customer drugged, then give them better stuff, etc.

Drugs Are Destroying Every Class and Ethnicity

The result is, that all across the de-industrialized section of the United States, it's not just black people and Hispanics who are buying drugs; it's also white folks. It's middle class Republicans, whose kids are dying with a needle in their arm. I'm telling you, this thing is going to change, if we use it right in a good way, if people actually think about it.

At the very end of Quinones' book, all these people in Ohio, for example, come to the realization that under Obama, nothing was going to change. In fact, Obama is in favor of drugs; he's in favor of total legalization. He's in favor of this whole crazy thing which is going on where we take a whole, huge part of the United States, except the coasts, and say, "OK, you're de-industrialized. There's nothing for you here. You've got a Wal-Mart, that's what you get. The rest of it is, you get on SSI (Supplemental Security Income) and you trade in pills, and you hook yourself to dope and that's your future." It was the outright revolt against this situation—being turned into vassals, essentially, in a plantation economy—that determined the 2016 election, and this revolt is still going on.

We have the unique perspective in our movement for showing people how an economy can work, and that can help reverse the otherwise hopeless despair that has swept through the former industrial powerhouse called the United States. I hope I have presented some form of challenge to the way you may have been thinking about all this. The idea is for you here to quickly figure out how you fit into this matrix that Lyndon LaRouche laid out in that old, old, but still young paper. Are you a professional organizer? Well then, you've got to really get steeped a lot more in Lyndon LaRouche's economics and meet his standards. You're free to do that, and we will support you in that endeavor.

Are you, on the other hand, that valuable person who actually understands something about productivity, but can't be a full-time organizer for whatever reasons, but would do anything to turn this country in the right direction? Will you help us do this? Will you volunteer whatever time you have, along with your passion and creativity? We really are throwing out a challenge here, very similar to the one that John F. Kennedy threw out to the entire American population, with his challenge to build a space program and get to the Moon. We have to do this; this nation has to survive. We're an essential part of any four-power agreement that you can think about. We have a unique history, most of which we've lost, but which is essential for the world. And failure is not an option here.

Recapturing Faith in Humanity

Question: Thank you so much. The world has changed. Not just that we're in another millennium with a 21st Century. This is not where it was 50 years ago when I was growing up, or 60 years ago, or 70. More people are educated; there are more professionals out there. More people are literate. There's something that has changed in the world *per se* that seems to offer a launch pad for changes which LaRouche is promoting—going back to what the American republic once stood for.

So, I was trying to think of using maybe the world almanac to identify those changes, but I think a lot of people see, a lot of liberals see the world as America, America in the history of post-World War II. But they don't see the world that LaRouche organizers have the capacity to see. I know we're not the only ones, but it does seem like most people have somehow lost the sense of mutuality, or faith in humanity that characterizes the values of LaRouche. It seems it might be useful to frame the need for change and renewal, or rediscovering values and so on, from that angle. Or, could you suggest something that LaRouche has written that I could look to, to help me frame something?

Boyd: Well, fundamentally, what LaRouche talks about, is creating that passion in every human being for the idea of immortality, if you will—the idea of living up to that God-given talent which we all have, called the creative spirit. That's his really most fundamental conception—inducing in other people the passion for discovery, for creativity, and for learning about other individuals, about other cultures, about all the other things that go with simple curiosity. I would submit to you that in many respects, Americans have lost curiosity; just pure curiosity. The idea of thinking about, wow, you're from another country; I'm really interested in that. What do you think? What do you believe? How do you interact with the world? What's your premise in terms of how you run your economy? What's your premise in terms of the social relations in your country?

If you recall, during periods of optimism in our country, during the space period for example, when I was growing up, there was a lot of interest in other areas of the world. People would get out their maps, they'd look at other countries. You'd be saying, what is that all about? I'm really interested in that, let's explore it.

I think Helga LaRouche's idea that you should adopt another country and make it sort of your own, is an excellent idea. Because then you can compare and think about how our culture differs from their culture. Is there a superior culture or are they all equivalent? I think LaRouche's answer to that would be, no, they're not all equivalent. In many respects, we here have lost that which made us unique in the first place. Which is the reason why we had a revolution against the British here, the scientifically advance, anti-oligarchical Western European culture, which our Constitution is founded on—all of those things which actually make America great, if you will, not some nostalgic idea about the 1950s, but that history which makes us great, we've lost touch with.

And with that history comes the notion of President John Quincy Adams that our role is not to go out and be the world's policeman. Our role is to lead by example as to the highest forms of civilization which ever existed. That doesn't mean sitting there and chanting out, "U.S.A.! U.S.A.! U.S.A.!" like mannequins. It was a highly intellectual culture which brought us the Constitution. The Constitution remains, probably, the highest instrument of law, more in line with natural law, than is found in any other place in the world.

I think if you want to read something LaRouche wrote which reflects the question you are asking, you should read or reread "The Coming Eurasian World," published in *EIR*, November 29, 2004. There he talks there about the relationships between cultures and what the role of the United States actually *should* be, based on our history, in the present international framework.

George Peter Alexander Healy, 1858
John Quincy Adams

this year. But more fundamental than stopping the coup, is getting the economic program implemented which will actually result in the 2016 vote being realized.

People are *desperate* out there, as you encountered. They see our solutions. What Lyndon LaRouche said in 2012 at his 90th birthday celebration was really quite remarkable. Go back and read it; he said that you have to get citizens to be citizens. They have to be able to take responsibility for the entire economy. There aren't these people in between the people and the government so you can play spectator sports with politics any more.

Our goal here is citizens, ready with pitchforks, demanding, "This is the program we want." That must be done with great passion. I have used the example of the space program, Kennedy's challenge to the American people. This is your mission at this point, to turn the United States back to our revolutionary foundations, if you will: Back to Hamilton, back to LaRouche, back to what we once were in the world. And that's really,— I think what you're going to find all over the place, as you go into these places, because these are the forgotten men and women of the United States, that they're ready to act.

China As a Mirror of the United States

Question: Hello, Barbara. I want to report on an upstate tour that I was on with three other organizers. It was a lot of fun. There was a high degree of recognition of Mr. LaRouche; a lot of the blue-collar folks up there could easily see the need to join the Belt and Road Initiative. When people could get their minds around the three pledges, and LaRouche's Four Laws, we saw great response from that; people signing up.

It was a lot of fun. The pamphlet was critically important in moving people and getting them signed up and at least initially thinking about what they could do to help this happen.

Boyd: I think you're going to find exactly that kind of response at this point in all of these places which are sort of the pivot counties. Most people recognize that the anti-Trump coup has really had a terrible, terrible, terrible impact, and has stalled and paralyzed all discussion. It is urgent that we communicate that this is for real, we can stop the coup, with the mid-term elections

Question: People were shocked, during our upstate tour, when we pointed their attention to the fact that China has developed very rapidly over the last 15 years. More than 800 million of their poorest people have been brought up out of dire poverty in the last 30 or so years. From 2013 to 2016, more than 55 million rural people were lifted out of poverty in China. At the same time, the United States has been engaged more and more in regime changes and bailouts: The juxtaposition of those two ideas really shocked people, in a good way.

Boyd: We've got to make the point to people that the same people who are running the coup against Trump, are the people who caused the deindustrialization of the United States, who sold us this bill of goods that Wall Street is where everything happens. We've got to get it so that whenever people hear that "ding, ding, ding, ding, ding," which is the constant background noise on the radio and everyplace else—announcing "this is how Wall Street did today"—they essentially say, "That's all bullshit, I don't want to hear it! I want to hear about the rising productivity levels in our population today; I want to hear about how we're actually creating systems of education which turn out responsible citizens. I want to hear about the level of scientific education in our population"—all of the standards that are implicit in what Lyndon LaRouche is talking about in the Four Laws.

That's what we've got to create in our population. When they hear that "ding, ding, ding, ding, ding," they should automatically react, "That's the ring of my funeral. I don't want to hear that anymore! I want to live!" And that's basically what we've got to do here.

LaRouche's Keen Insights in the 1970s

Question: I want to bring up a couple things from what Barbara was saying and my reflections on that.

In 1974 through 1975, approximately an 18-month period, Lyndon LaRouche created the Fusion Energy Foundation. In 1975 he wrote a pamphlet called *How the International Development Bank Will Work*. That same year he wrote a paper called "The Emergency Employment Act" of 1975. What's relevant was not what he was writing, but what we were doing at the time, because that period saw the most extensive expansion of our organization in our history.

We went from being an almost entirely campus-based organization to being a street-based organization, which was organizing at plant gates and at unemployment centers and at intersections, and eventually at airports and things like that; but we did it over a period of basically 18 months. We went from having maybe 9 or 10 centers in the United States, to being active in over 50 cities in the United States. We were actually at one point publishing our newspaper, *New Solidarity*, not once a week, not twice a week, but even three times a week. That was only for a short period of time, but we did it. We had an idea about what we called "multiplier factors." We talked about the idea that if you had a newspaper that went out to somebody, the multiplier factor of the number of people reading a copy was about 7 or 8.

At that time in the United States, you could actually find plant gates and you could go to shift changes, and you could talk to 5,000 workers at Chevy Gear and Axle in Detroit, and then hit the Dodge Main plant which was down the road; and you didn't have to do much except pick up your bundle of papers and walk over to it. You sometimes would get chased away from the plant gates, and had to somehow do some other things—it was not all an entirely benign environment.

But the important point is, this idea of a small force suddenly creating a turmoil, an intellectual turmoil in the United States that could create hegemony for an idea that had not been known before. In other words, you just seize a moment, you take an idea that people had never heard before, but within a period of months, they have been caused to confront it. But that's not just by a shock effect. You have to educate. You said a few things earlier about the idea of this. And I just want for you, Barbara, to say a few more things about this idea.

I don't know if you have any reflections on the particulars of what I said, but I think this area of discussion that you introduced is an important one to go back to, because what we're talking about here is the idea of cadre organization, meaning, centralized, professional organizers, and then the larger phase.

Boyd: Sure. I think there's a certain point at which that whole, what I'll call a standard, within our organization suffered. Back then, LaRouche insisted that our professional organizers had to be able to function as epistemological warriors. And that means they had to take on the very personal responsibility of really thinking through his Dialectical Economics course, which was a much tougher course in most respects than anything we are presenting today. Before you even started talking to others about his economic concepts, Lyndon LaRouche expected you to read through the works of German critical philosophy, to study Plato, and to read through the great thinkers in human history.

In his view, it was through that exercise that he could prove to you that his economic concepts were a fundamental advance not only in economics, but also in the overall epistemology of how thinking and mind are understood by human beings.

Today, we have to think about this business of education a little bit differently in some respects. We're not necessarily looking for the person who agrees with us right away; the person that we may be looking for is the person who may disagree with us right away. When you engage people in political dialogue, you are looking for that person who shows a certain toughness of mind, if you will, a certain healthy skepticism, an individuality, a

We're not necessarily looking for the person who agrees with us right away ... who may disagree with us. When you engage people in political dialogue, you are looking for that person who shows a certain toughness of mind, a healthy skepticism, an individuality, a person who says, "OK, if you can convince me, I'll be on your side, but you've got to prove it." That's a tough mind.

EIRNS

Labor Committee organizers (right and left) at the Fruehauf strike in North Carolina in July, 1971.

person who says, "OK, if you can convince me, I'll be on your side, but you've got to prove it." That's a tough mind.

Lyndon LaRouche's view is that if you actually understand what he's talking about in terms of economics, if you really, really get it, then you have become someone who can withstand any kind of political battle and won't fall apart. Should somebody come at you and try to disorganize you or whatever, you're going to stand by what you believe and what you know. And the most important thing is, *don't say something you don't know*.

So much of what goes on in the United States today is based on opinion: "I have this opinion," or "I have this shtick, or "I have that shtick." If you're really rooted in what LaRouche is talking about, you've got to actually understand that you don't go out and talk about things which you can't really know. You stick to what you know, and then you basically expand from there into things you

don't know, out of this wonderful thing which I'll call creative discovery or curiosity, a lot of which we've lost in our dumbed-down society.

And sometimes, you are not able to get across a lot of what we're talking about by simplifying it. Sometimes simplification is a very elegant way to actually express something. But most of the time, you have to be patient enough and strong enough to put people through the full ropes of grappling with the ideas that Lyndon LaRouche laid out.

What always happens when you are in a room, waiting to meet with Lyndon LaRouche? You know you aren't going to have an easy ride during the conversation—ever! Many times he starts out by punning you to death, giving you a whole bunch of puns, to see if your mind is loose enough to actually think creatively. A lot of his puns are really bad. You tolerate that. But it certainly does loosen you up, and you find yourself thinking in a different way.

That is his personality: He views political organizing essentially as dialogue with somebody, having a dialogue with you. And the purpose of the dialogue is to lift your mind to a place where you haven't been before. It's not to roll around in your prejudices or play them, or manipulate them. He wants to take you to a place which is called being human. It's called actually having the highest level of thinking. And if I can get you to that place, then we're off and running in terms of getting you to act on these principles.

Take No One for Granted, Think Like Beethoven

If you reflect on how LaRouche organizes, he never takes anybody for granted.

Everyone's unique; and LaRouche is in there, when he's organizing to say, "How is your mind working? I want to find that out. And then I want to figure out how I can elevate your mind." Now that takes skill; that takes all of the things we do in the LaRouche movement today. If you're good at music and understand Beethoven, then you understand the central concepts of organizing, you understand the freedom/necessity paradox, which Lyndon LaRouche talked about endlessly, in terms of creativity.

And that's the reason he had us all listen to and study Beethoven in the first place—to get us to understand

Lyndon LaRouche's view is that if you actually understand what he's talking about in terms of economics, if you really, really get it, then you have become someone who can withstand any kind of political battle and won't fall apart. Should somebody come at you and try to disorganize you, you're going to stand by what you believe and what you know. And the most important thing is, *don't say something you don't know.*

how that works at the deepest levels of the human soul. You need to use every single tool that you can pull in. You use choral work, you use poetry, you use science, to lift yourself up and lift up that human being before you. Then you—and the person with whom you are engaged—can think differently than when your encounter began. That's your purpose, that's what's called polemical organizing.

It's very easy to fall into a different type of organizing which is called pragmatism, i.e., you and I agree, and we have the same thoughts about X, and therefore, you're going to agree to do something for me, or I'm going to agree to do something for you. It doesn't change the person. LaRouche's fundamental orientation in building this organization is, I want to change how people think. And the inherently creative person, the one I'm looking for—the ones and twos— who have this idea and passion in them already, I'm going to take and turn them into the type of tough intellectuals who will be able to carry forward this program to others by having that core mission-orientation of: I'm going to do this no matter what, no matter what comes in my way, I'm going to get it done.

LaRouche often talked about the educational process he set in motion in creating an organization from scratch, saying that the criteria for leadership in his organization have to include having done something fundamentally new, as a contribution to some intellectual field, something truly creative—that leadership requires that. That's what he holds up as the quality that a leader has to have—an active, fruitful creative orientation.

He was very tough in building this organization, and his emphasis was on education and on something I'll call "polemical education," that is, the idea is to go in, figure out what the governing axioms are of somebody, in terms of how they're looking at the world, and if their axioms are wrong, figure out how to get underneath their skin and cause them to change. That's the challenge of everything I was talking about before: how to create an organization, how to forge a group of organizers who are capable of doing that. And the only model I know of, that's ever been done successfully in recent history, is Lyndon LaRouche's creation of the National Caucus of Labor Committees.

The Hypotheses Underlying Lyndon LaRouche's Four Laws and the World Land-Bridge

by William F. Wertz, Jr.

The following article is an adaptation of a speech given on January 6, 2018 to an audience in Oakland, California.

May 15—I have found that in many cases there is an insufficient understanding of Lyndon LaRouche's Four Laws, and in some cases a tendency to pragmatically reduce the Four Laws to a lifeless four-point formula. In some cases there is a tendency to cherry-pick one or another of the Four Laws— for example, to emphasize only the First Law, a return to Glass-Steagall, or only to support the Fourth Law, the urgent development of fusion power. In one case that I am aware of, a resolution was introduced into a state legislature which focused exclusively on the First and Second Laws (Glass-Steagall and national banking), omitting the Third and Fourth Laws. In other cases, two resolutions have been simultaneously introduced into the same legislature—one supporting Glass-Steagall alone, and one supporting the Four Laws as a whole, with the implied assessment that Glass-Steagall alone might have a greater chance to be adopted.

What all of these approaches reflect, in varying degrees, is a failure to see Lyndon LaRouche's Four Laws as one coherent living principle, an anti-entropic, self-subsisting positive conception of the necessity of the self-expansion of human labor power in the form of creative mentation. In many cases, such approaches reflect

propitiation of the prevailing false axiomatic assumptions of the very Anglo-Dutch liberal imperial system, which the Four Laws as a whole are designed to challenge and replace.

Challenging False Axioms

Properly understood, the Four Laws polemically challenge those false axiomatic assumptions, which stand in the way of human progress. As necessary as the re-enactment of Glass-Steagall is, it alone will not solve the problem. For example, the separation of commercial banking and speculative banking existed even in Mussolini's Italy. Glass-Steagall, without national banking, without a scientific conception of productive investment of credit, and without the concept of the necessity of generating a higher-order economic platform, will solve nothing.

President Trump has endorsed Glass-Steagall and the American System of Economics, but does he support the Second Law, national banking? He references Alexander Hamilton, but at the same time he supports Andrew Jackson, who dismantled the National Bank, which was and is an essential aspect of Alexander Hamilton's American System.

The Third Law, credit for increased productivity, is even more controversial. Neither the advocates of Milton Friedman in the Republican Party, nor of John Maynard Keynes in the Democratic Party, have any scientific conception of productivity. The Republicans are insistent on balancing the budget, and the Democrats, with their Green ideology, are opposed to precisely those technologies which are productive and thus would contribute to the necessary anti-entropic development of the economy.

With respect to the Fourth Law, not only is there an inadequate appreciation of the need to develop a higher-order economic-cultural platform as represented by the development of fusion power and the exploration of space, but there is a concerted effort to prevent such a development. After all, shouldn't we rather concentrate on more appropriate technologies like solar and wind power, and the recycling of dog poop? Doesn't such an emphasis encourage false technological optimism in violation of the law of entropy? Shouldn't we rather focus on solving our problems here on Earth?

The Underlying Hypotheses

Today I will address the underlying hypotheses involved in Lyndon LaRouche's proposed Four Laws and in the policy of the World Land-Bridge, because if we are to succeed, we must understand the revolutionary ideas which generated this policy, and simultaneously examine those false axiomatic assumptions that stand in the way of its implementation, unless deci-

from a painting by Ezra Ames

Alexander Hamilton

sively rejected.

The Four Laws are not just four points. There's a matter of principle involved in them, and what I hope to do today is to provoke you to think about what exactly that principle is, because it's the fundamental principle of human progress. It involves the Sublime as defined by Friedrich Schiller. It also involves hypothesizing higher hypotheses as defined by Plato. Those two concepts, Schiller's notion of the Sublime and Hypothesizing the Higher Hypothesis, are the operative principles behind the Four Laws that you have to understand if you're going to understand what's entailed in the world that we have to create, looking into the future.

The illustration of the World Land-Bridge that appears on the cover of the new pamphlet produced by the LaRouche Political Action Committee, *LaRouche's Four Laws for Economic Recovery*, is highly suggestive. It depicts a specific angle, which is not the typical angle or the typical view of the World Land-Bridge. When I first saw this, it immediately brought to my mind Michelangelo's *Creation of Adam* on the ceiling of the Sistine Chapel in Rome. As you can see, the North American land mass is represented as an arm extending toward the Eurasian arm, and what you have is a gap, the Bering Strait, between those two extensions. Unfortunately, Michelangelo is very oriented toward muscles and not brains; and, of course, he depicts the Creator as a muscular human figure creating a muscular human being, Adam, as opposed to the notion of the Creator who creates man in his own living image as a creative being.

This latter conception is that of the new Adam as depicted in Raphael's *Transfiguration*, which also appears in the Vatican.

In a certain sense, the contrast between these two paintings embodies the task which we have before us of creating a new paradigm in which a new man, as a creative species, is able to emerge in the world. The World Land-Bridge has a defi-

Milton Friedman

John Maynard Keynes

Creation of Adam, from a fresco by Michelangelo on the Sistine Chapel's ceiling in the Vatican.

nite, necessary physical-technological aspect—however, that is not primary, but rather, what is primary is the creativity necessary to create it and the increase in human creativity generated by its creation.

Creativity and the Sublime

In *I Corinthians* 15:45, the Apostle Paul wrote: "The first man, Adam, became a living being; the last Adam (which is Christ), a life-giving spirit." The word for "spirit" in Greek is *pneuma*. The point is that the new man is not just alive, but is life-giving for others. Another translation of *pneuma* is creative fire; and of course, in the *Transfiguration*, Christ as he is transfigured, is engulfed in light which is meant to represent creative fire or intellect. In distinction to Christ who is creative fire, some of the Apostles who are with him on the mount are actually blinded by the light and recoil from the announcement that Christ is the Son of God.

At the base of the mount, a boy is pictured who is in some way incapacitated, and the other Apostles pictured there are unable to cure him because they lack faith in the creative power embodied by Christ, who later cures the boy when he descends from the mount. Eventually, the Apostles, to the extent that they stop recoiling and embrace Christ as the manifestation of the Logos, or creative reason, develop that capability on their own.

In *I Corinthians* 15, Paul continues: "For since death came through a human being, the resurrection of the dead came also through a human being, or just as in Adam all died, so too in Christ shall all be brought to life." Nicholas of Cusa in his *On Learned Ignorance* makes the point that a whole resurrected man is an intellect; and in one of his essays, *On Searching for God*, Cusa writes: "Our intellectual spirit has the power of fire in itself.

The *Transfiguration* conveys the power of creative reason, and it is that power which is the basis for transforming the face of the Earth through the Eurasian Land-Bridge, including a tunnel or bridge across the Bering Strait. It's through this process that we actually get to the point where man can be truly man, that is, he can actually be in the living image of the Creator and act on his capacity for creativity.

Multiply-connected Universal Physical Principles

The reason I'm starting in this way, is that Lyndon LaRouche wrote the following in an article entitled, "Who Needs Brains, When We Have Muscles?":

"[T]he root definition of grand strategy lies in the multiply-connected character of two sets of universal principles.... [T]hese are,

The Transfiguration, the last painting by Raphael.

respectively, sets of universal physical principles, and also sets of universal principles of social relations, the latter typified by the greatest works of Classical artistic composition. The multiple-connectedness among these two sets of universal principles, defines the means by which mankind increases our species' power in and over the physical universe, and also the means of co-operation by which that physical power is developed and effectively applied."

LaRouche has emphasized particularly in his book, *Earth's Next Fifty Years*, and in *The Coming Eurasian World* that ridding the planet of the Anglo-Dutch liberal tradition is the absolute precondition for preserving civilization.

Thus, the issue before us is not just defeating an attempted coup by British intelligence and the British Empire against the Presidency of the United States. If we are going to succeed in implementing the Eurasian Land-Bridge and in enacting LaRouche's Four Laws, a much larger issue must be addressed.

Edgar Allan Poe: the Pathway to Truth

The American poet Edgar Allan Poe wrote a short story called "Mellonta Tauta" which gets at the crux of the issue. Poe writes there that if you believe that there are only two pathways to truth, empiricism and logical deduction, then your mind will be controlled by the oligarchy, by imperial forces, because neither of those forms of mentation is valid—neither empiricism, which is based on sense perception, nor logical deduction, which assumes certain fixed categories of thought from which the human mind is only capable of coming to logical deductions. If you accept that, then there's

Nicholas of Cusa (1402-1464)

Edgar Allen Poe

no place for creativity, which is the actual condition of mankind as the sole creative species that we know of in the Universe.

Poe says that if you believe that the only way the mind functions is through empiricism and logical deduction, then you are reduced to a condition of merely creeping and crawling. In contrast, he says that the actual nature of mankind is to soar through what he calls conjectures, through hypothesis, and he cites Johannes Kepler, the person who discovered the principle of universal gravitation, as an exemplar of this method of hypothesis, which should be characteristic of all human beings.

This is important, because unless you yourself examine the assumptions underlying the way you think, you are subject to being controlled by the Anglo-Dutch liberal system even as you deny such a thing even exists. How many people have said that the British Empire is not really functional any longer, that the Queen, her consort Philip and her son Prince Charles have no power? How many people accept without question that if there is an empire it is the United States of America, which is a deliberately false construction spread by the British Empire?

The way that empire operates is by controlling the way you think; that's the significance of Poe's short story—he understood that. He was an American patriot who understood that in the early 1800s. This was also understood by the leaders of the European Renaissance.

Nicholas of Cusa, for example, argues that when the Apostle Paul said that he was raptured into the Third Heaven during his Damascus Road conversion, he was transported into the realm of creative reason, thus transcending the First Heaven, sense perception, and the Second Heaven, logical deduction.

Rembrandt: Can You See?

One of the best examples of this understanding is Rembrandt's *Aristotle Contemplating the Bust of Homer*.

Of course, Aristotle is the leading philosopher who promoted logical deduction based on sense perception. In other words, the categories from which you deduce conclusions logically, ultimately come from sense perception, and according to Aristotle, human beings are trapped in this self-reflexive theorem lattice without access to creativity.

In his painting, Rembrandt directly attacks this central Aristotelian conception. If you look closely at this painting, it is Aristotle who is blind intellectually; whereas Homer, who was physically blind, is the person capable of vision. Rembrandt gets across Aristotle's empiricism by having him put his hand on the head of Homer, as if through sense perception he's going to solve the mystery, for him, of what allowed Homer to be a creative poet.

This same issue was addressed in the *The School of Athens* by Raphael. Many argue that Aristotle is just a continuation of Plato, that he was actually a student of Plato, and in that capacity completed the work of Plato—but Raphael ironically makes it very clear that Aristotle and Plato are diametrically opposed. The figure with his hand point-

'Aristotle Contemplating a Bust of Homer,' by Rembrandt (1653).

ing up to the heavens is Plato. He is carrying his book in his hand, the *Timaeus*, and the *Timaeus* is a discussion of creation. Aristotle, on the other hand, has his hand pointed downward towards the ground, and he is carrying his book, *The Ethics*. The book is leaning on his leg, so if he moves, the book will fall to the ground.

Fight Aristotle: Fight Slavery

In *The Ethics*, Aristotle puts forth a defense of slavery, whereas in the *Timaeus*, the conception is that each human being is capable of creative reason and that's the basis for creation. What Raphael is doing here is demolishing the false notion that Aristotle was in the tradition of Plato, when in fact he denied creativity and Plato's conception that man participates in eternal ideas.

Many people say, "Well, the British Empire is not militarily strong; it doesn't physically occupy countries in the way it did during the 1800s and even into the 20th century." But that's not how imperialism works. Fundamentally, imperialism operates from the standpoint of control of the mind.

You have to examine your assumptions, and also examine the assumptions of other people. I would say the vast majority of American citizens and many throughout the world do not do that, they do not examine their axiomatic assumptions, and therefore they're controlled by the very

Detail from Raphael's 'School of Athens' shows Plato (left) and Aristotle.

British Empire agent Parson Thomas Malthus.

Charles Darwin

H.G. Wells

Halford Mackinder

system which they deny exists.

The British Empire of Slavery

Think about the effects, for instance, of Parson Thomas Malthus. Today, the ideology which has become prevalent within the West is the argument that industry is destroying the environment, and human techno- logical activity is creating climate change to the detriment of animals and the planet Earth.

Thomas Malthus was British and he was an instru- ment of British imperial policy, including in India, and his argument was against population growth. He said that agriculture can only grow arithmetically, but human population grows exponentially; therefore, you have to reduce population—and of course, by exten- sion, you also have to reduce technological develop- ment. That's one of the ways in which people are con- trolled. Thomas Malthus was an agent of the British Empire, and he operates to this day within the minds of our fellow citizens and policy-makers.

Look at Charles Darwin, another agent of the Brit- ish Empire, who enunciated a false notion of evolu- tion based on the notion of survival of the fittest; whereas, in fact, the evolutionary development of life is actually brought about not by the survival of the fit-

test, but by an unfolding of what is latent in the creative process of the Universe in the first place. Evolution is actu- ally based on love and reason combined, not competition. All you have to do is look at the human species and how it has evolved—not bio- logically, but how it has evolved socially; it is through reason and love for mankind and for the truth that results in scientific breakthroughs, or what are called hypotheses, which can then be technologically implemented to the benefit of all mankind.

Malthus and Darwin are two British pseudo- thinkers, actually propagandists, who continue to this day to control the thinking of most Ameri- cans in one way or the other.

Or, look at Adam Smith: The American Rev- olution was fought against the free trade doctrine as espoused by Adam Smith in his book, *The Wealth of Nations*, and yet, an entire spectrum of political life in our country still adheres to the idea espoused by Adam Smith to enslave the col- onies—free trade.

The American Revolution Opposed Adam Smith

At the same time, you have others who adhere to the views of a later British so-called economist, John Maynard Keynes. In a very real way, the Republican and Democratic Parties are divided between these two British ideologues—Smith and Keynes—who put for- ward two bogus conceptions of so-called economics, in opposition to the American System of economics, in order to effectively trap Americans, among others, in this intellectual prison of empiricism and logical de- duction.

Other British ideologues in the service of Empire include Bertrand Russell and H.G. Wells. Bertrand Russell, the pacifist who proposed to carry out a pre- emptive nuclear strike on the then Soviet Union, and proudly proclaimed that he was not a Christian based

Prince Philip, husband and consort of Queen Elizabeth II.

Prince Bernhard, consort of Queen Juliana of the Netherlands.

War, or what we call the French and Indian Wars. And at that point, the British East India Company took over large portions of India and eventually China: It was an empire based on a private corporation with its own army.

Although the British East India Company and its partner in crime, the Dutch East India Company, no longer exist as corporate entities, the model persists. Take for instance the World Wildlife Fund.

In 1961 Prince Bernhard of the Netherlands, i.e., the Dutch, founded the World Wildlife Fund (WWF). He was its first president. Prince Philip became the president of the British branch of the World Wildlife Fund in 1961, and continued in that position through 1982; he functioned as the president of the World Wildlife Fund International from 1981 until 1996. Now he's president emeritus of the World Wildlife Fund. And what is this? It's the core of the environmentalist movement, a Malthusian, genocidal, anti-human movement that has taken over the thinking of institutions and of people throughout the world.

This Anglo-Dutch system persists and continues to define the prevailing false axiomatic assumptions of thought in the United States and elsewhere.

on the alleged crimes perpetrated in the name of Christianity, which pale in comparison to his own.

H.G. Wells' *Open Conspiracy* put forward the conception of globalization, in opposition to the principle of national sovereignty. His conception was the precursor to Tony Blair's justification for regime change under the guise of the "Responsibility to Protect," a policy implemented by successive U.S. Presidents.

Look as well at Halford Mackinder, who developed the British Empire's Russophobic notion of geopolitics.

Or, look back a little further at John Locke (1632-1704), who in contrast to the American Declaration of Independence, which called for the Leibnizian idea of "life, liberty and the pursuit of happiness," put forward the opposite conception which is the basis for slavery, as in the case of Aristotle, of "life, liberty and property."

The Axioms of the Anglo-Dutch Empire of Slavery

The point I'm making here, is how does the British Empire, or the Anglo-Dutch system, control the way we think? It is through these kinds of false axiomatic assumptions, which assumptions the victim firmly defends as if they were his very own.

The Anglo-Dutch liberal system came into power in 1763, with the Treaty of Paris, after the Seven Years'

The Elephant Hiding in the Middle of the Room

In his book, *Earth's Next Fifty Years*, Lyndon LaRouche called this the elephant defecating on the bed of the honeymoon couple. The reason I'm raising this is because the new paradigm of the World Land-Bridge will not prevail if the world does not rid itself of this Anglo-Dutch liberal system. We have to rid ourselves of the false axiomatic assumptions of this system, otherwise, we will be controlled to our self-destruction by that same Anglo-Dutch imperial system, which we are told doesn't exist.

This is crucial. It is crucial in terms of the battle for the World Land-Bridge. It is crucial in terms of the fight to implement Lyndon LaRouche's Four Laws.

The Four Laws are a total assault on the false axiomatic assumptions of the Anglo-Dutch liberal system. And the only way to succeed is to understand that, as the Apostle Paul was told, it is necessary to kick against the pricks.

Now, let me address Lyndon LaRouche's Four Laws from the standpoint of Friedrich Schiller's Sublime, and Plato's Hypothesizing the Higher Hypothesis.

Hypothesizing the Higher Hypothesis

As I have stated, the Four Laws are not merely four points. The Four Laws are not an objective four-point program. You have to look at the operative principle: It's a living principle of the universe, which is expressed in these Four Laws, and as such it's also an expression of the living Constitutional principle of the Preamble of the American Constitution. The Preamble says, "We, the People of the United States, in order to form a more perfect Union, establish Justice, ensure domestic Tranquility, provide for the common defense, promote the General Welfare, and secure the Blessings of Liberty to ourselves and our Posterity, do ordain and establish this Constitution for the United States of America."

Now, look at LaRouche's Four Laws. The first law is "the immediate re-enactment of the Glass-Steagall law, as instituted by Franklin Roosevelt back in 1933, without modification as to principle of action." And the fundamental thing that the Glass-Steagall law does, is it makes a distinction between productive investment that promotes the general welfare, the common defense, and other principles of the Preamble of the Constitution, and speculative, predatory activity. Specifically, the original Banking Act of 1933 (the Glass-Steagall Act) is an "Act to provide for the safer and more effective use of the assets of banks, to regulate interbank control, to prevent the undue diversion of funds into speculative operations, and for other purposes."

The Glass-Steagall law is based on the constitutional principle that the only investors who are defended are those who contribute to principles as defined by the Preamble of the Constitution; that is contributing to the well-being of the population, and its continuing advancement, as opposed to speculative activity.

LaRouche's second law is, "A return to a system of top-down, and thoroughly defined as National Bank-ing," as we had under Alexander Hamilton. We had a version of that under Abraham Lincoln with the greenback policy, and we also had a version of that policy under Franklin Roosevelt during the 1930s. But, the nation has not had such a national banking system during a great part of our history. But when we have had such a national banking system, credit has been generated for the purpose of promoting the general welfare.

Credit Is Not Money: It's the Future

How that credit should be extended is fundamentally a voluntaristic notion. It's based on the fact that mankind can extend credit, and if mankind extends credit for productive activity, then mankind is actually enhancing the further development of the human species and of the population of the country—"We, the People ..."

With respect to the Third Law, LaRouche writes, "The purpose of the use of a Federal Credit-system is to generate high-productivity trends in improvements of employment, with the accompanying intention to increase the physical-economic productivity and standard of living of the persons and households of the United States ... by reliance on the essential human principle, which distinguishes the human personality from the systematic characteristics of the lower forms of life ..." So, again, you have here, the distinction between man, as creative, and lower forms of life.

The next portion of LaRouche's third law I think is most significant: "The ceaseless increase of the physical-productivity of employment, accompanied by its benefits for the general welfare, are a principle of Federal law, which must be a paramount standard of achievement of the nation and the individual. Every individual in society has the right derived from natural law, to pursue happiness, to participate in the uniquely human process of upward anti-entropic growth, the creation of a higher platform of society to bequeath the next generation."

So the idea here is coherent, as Lyndon LaRouche says, with the principle of perfectibility embedded in Federal law. The Preamble says that "We, the People, in order to form a more perfect Union ..." So again, you're dealing here with anti-entropic improvements in employment, in order to enhance the general welfare. And I think the further point here, is the creation of a "higher platform of society, to bequeath the next generation."

Here we are discussing the question of anti-entropic growth "for our posterity."

Anti-Entropic Growth

This notion of a platform is something I'm going to come back to, in terms of Platonic hypothesizing.

LaRouche's fourth law is: "'Adopt a Fusion-Driver 'Crash Program.' The essential distinction of man from all lower forms of life, hence, in practice, is that it presents the means for the perfection of the specifically affirmative aims and needs of human individual and social life…. A fusion economy is the presently urgent next step and standard for man's gains of power within the Solar system, and, later, beyond."

Thus, the Four Laws are not just four points of a minimal four-point program. They're also not in isolation from one another. You cannot advocate Glass-Steagall, without National Banking, or without creating a higher-order economic-cultural platform for society as a whole based on a scientific concept of productivity, and without emphasizing the frontiers of science, including fusion power and space exploration.

So, in a very real sense, this is a challenge to all of the false axiomatic assumptions of the Anglo-Dutch liberal system, the zero-growth conception that I went through earlier. Lyndon LaRouche is talking about the "ceaseless increase of the physical-productivity of employment." This notion runs against the conception that the universe is entropic. It runs against all of the green ideology, and all of the Keynesian ideology, neither of which make any distinction between productive and nonproductive forms of investment. And it rejects the entire free-trade dogma of Adam Smith, because what it's putting forward is that man can and must, voluntaristically, based on reason and his love for his fellow man, commit himself to an economic policy which promotes the general welfare *of all*.

With the Four Laws you have a coherent statement of fundamental principle, of man's relationship to the entire Solar System and the Universe, the same princi-

Friedrich Schiller
(1759-1805)

ple that is embedded in the Preamble to the U.S. Constitution.

Schiller: The Love of Mankind

Now, the basic thesis that I want to develop is the following: This love of mankind is the issue of the Sublime, as defined by Schiller; it's also the issue of Hypothesizing the Higher Hypothesis of Plato, and it's also the concept of Prometheus. This notion is reflected in the contrast between the *Creation of Adam* by Michelangelo and the *Transfiguration* by Raphael, that is, the contrast between the first Adam and the last Adam. In contrast to the false axiomatic assumptions of the Anglo-Dutch liberal system, which is the enemy of such progress, there is a consistent principle, as expressed artistically in Classical art, which is the Principle of the Sublime, the Principle of Hypothesizing the Higher Hypothesis, and at the same time the Principle of Prometheus.

As you know, Prometheus gave man fire. Remember what I quoted from Nicholas of Cusa earlier. He said, "Our intellectual spirit has the power of fire in itself." Remember also the quote from Paul in Corinthians, "the last Adam, a life-giving creative fire," or "spirit"—that's the nature of man. And that is what has brought about advances in human society throughout history, to the extent mankind has been able to defeat various forms of imperial rule, the current expression of which is the Anglo-Dutch/British liberal system.

The Gift of Prometheus

Prometheus gave man fire, in opposition to Zeus, who was the embodiment of the imperial system: Zeus did not want mankind to be educated, to be able to develop his creativity. Zeus wanted slaves, as did Aristotle, and nothing more, because slaves are easy to control. So he denied creativity, whereas Prometheus gave man not only fire, physical fire, but he also gave man a method of thinking, which is the Platonic method of hypothesizing, as Edgar Allan Poe describes that in "Mellonta Tauta."

Specifically, there's a dialogue called the *Philebus* by Plato, in which he says:

> There is a gift of the gods—so at least it seems evident to me—which they let fall from their abode, and it was through Prometheus, or one like him, that it reached mankind, together with a fire exceeding bright. The men of old, who were better than ourselves and dwelt nearer the gods, passed on this gift in the form of a saying. All things, so it ran, that are ever said to be consist of a one and a many, and have in their nature a conjunction of limit and unlimitedness.

Now, there are two ways to understand that conjunction: The one is to view it from the standpoint of the imposition of a limit upon the unlimited. Lyndon LaRouche, in his 1994 paper, "The Truth About Temporal Eternity," states,

> If the human species were to adopt any fixed hypotheses as permanent, that commitment would lead toward the extinction of the human species. Fixed modes of human productive and related behavior, must lead toward an entropic collapse of the human species.

The alternative conception, developed by Plato in his *Philebus*, is that there can be a conjunction of the limited and unlimited, in which you have an unlimited family of higher-order limits. And this is the conception of Higher Hypothesis, also presented in his *Republic*. In other words, given a certain mode of production, that mode of production is a certain kind of economic-cultural platform, and that hypothesis defines the economic activities, the resources, and so forth, upon which that mode of production is based. If you stay in that one mode of production, mankind will experience entropy and he will be destroyed.

Any Fixed Hypotheses Will Lead to Extinction

So, what's required? What's required is the development of a higher-order hypothesis: The conception of an unlimited succession of limits, of hypotheses that redefine the entire theorem lattice. This would be the equivalent of going from a mode of production based on burning wood, to a mode of production based on coal or oil; or nuclear fission, or fusion. So, in a very real sense, this conception of developing a higher-order economic platform is Plato's conception of Higher Hypotheses.

What we're talking about here, is the concept developed by LaRouche in his Third and Fourth Laws, the creation of a higher-order anti-entropic platform based on fusion power and space exploration, an expression of the necessity of developing higher-order hypotheses to overcome the apparent "limits to growth" in a society based on a single, fixed hypothesis that defines its social and economic activity.

A further point here is increasing the rate of what LaRouche calls "potential relative population density": The true metric for economy being man's power over and in nature, through higher-order hypotheses that represent scientific breakthroughs that allow mankind to apply new, more productive technologies, on behalf of man's general welfare.

The point I would make, is that Plato's conception of the capacity to hypothesize higher hypotheses constitutes the basis for increasing the rate of potential relative population density, because you're increasing the power of the average individual over nature, through this capacity to hypothesize higher-order hypotheses.

LaRouche's Four Laws express this conception of hypothesizing higher hypotheses in behalf of promoting the general welfare of all the people. This is a Promethean conception, as developed by Plato. It is the method of thinking of Prometheus, not just the gift of physical fire.

Prometheus Did Not Regret His Deed

It is also Schiller's notion of the Sublime. Schiller wrote two articles on the Sublime, in the earlier of which he puts forward the notion that Prometheus is sublime. He writes: "Prometheus was sublime. Since put in chains in the Caucasus, he did not regret his deed and did not confess that he was wrong."

It is this Promethean conception of man, in which man soars, in which man engages in hypothesizing the higher hypothesis—which is the conception of man, the new man, under the New Paradigm, which we have to be committed to building, in opposition to the false axiomatic assumptions which control us otherwise, which are an expression of the Anglo-Dutch liberal imperial system.

This conception of the Sublime is expressed by Friedrich Schiller in his play, *The Virgin of Orleans*,

Joan of Arc

about Joan of Arc. Schiller's point is that as in the case of Christ, man—in this case a woman—even in dying is free, insofar as he or she is making a willful decision, based on his or her love of mankind, and the love of truth, to make a contribution to the future of mankind, to man's posterity—and that's what Joan of Arc did. She fought the British, the Normans who were entrenched in northern France, and were trying to take over all of France. As a result of her efforts, the first nation state in human history was created in France under Louis XI. And at the end of the play, Schiller says, "Brief is the pain, the joy shall be eterne!"

Beethoven and Joan of Arc

That's the conception of the Sublime. Her situation was similar to that of Prometheus, who in *Prometheus Bound* was bound on a rock by Zeus, for eternity—where an eagle ate his liver, as a means of torturing him, to try to get him to give up, to confess that he was wrong, to not continue with his contribution to mankind.

You have a similar situation with Beethoven: Beethoven, at the age of 28, was already becoming

deaf. In the year 1802, he wrote his "Heiligenstadt Testament" for his relatives:

> For my brothers Carl and [Johann] Beethoven
> … Ah, it seemed to me impossible to leave the world until I had brought forth all that I felt was within me. … I hope my determination will remain firm to endure until it pleases the inexorable Parcae [that's the Fates] to break the thread. Perhaps I shall get better, perhaps not; I am ready. — Forced to become a philosopher already in my twenty-eighth year, — oh it is not easy, and for the artist much more difficult than for anyone else. — Divine One, thou seest my inmost soul, thou knowest that therein dwells the love of mankind and the desire to do good. … Recommend virtue to your children; it alone, not money, can make them happy. I speak from experience; this was what upheld me in time of misery. … — With joy I hasten to meet death. — … Come when thou wilt, I shall meet thee bravely.

The attitude expressed here by Beethoven reminds one of Shakespeare's comment, in his play *Julius Caesar,* that "A coward dies a thousand times before his death, but the valiant taste of death but once."

J.S. Bach's Passions

You have the same principle expressed in Bach's *St. John Passion* where, after Christ is crucified, an alto sings an absolutely powerful aria, bringing to the fore this sublime conception. In translation, she sings:

> It is fulfilled!
> All hope for every ailing spirit!
> The night of grief
> Is now its final hours counting.
> The hero of Judah wins with might
> And ends the fight.
> It is fulfilled!

Initially she echoes Christ, "It is fulfilled!" But then suddenly she breaks from the night of grief into a new paradigm. She sings joyfully: "The hero of Judah wins with might and ends the fight." One of the works of music which Lyndon LaRouche has cited, particularly, reflecting his understanding of the importance of Prometheus, is Brahms's *Four Serious Songs*, which culminates in the final song based on *I Corinthians* 13. "Though I speak with the tongues of men and of angels, and have not charity, I am become as sounding brass or tinkling cymbal." Which then concludes: "And now abideth Faith, Hope, and Charity, these three. But the greatest of these is Charity."

All of human progress has been based upon this Promethean conception, a conception of the Sublime, contributing to posterity knowing full well that we all die, and yet, remaining true to one's love of mankind, and love of Truth, even in the face of death, as Christ did and Joan of Arc did—and as Beethoven did.

Beethoven: Every Man Becomes a Brother

Beethoven wrote the "Heiligenstadt Testament" in 1802. He wrote his *Ninth Symphony* between the years 1822 and 1824. Think of the gift that that represents to mankind! This is the setting of Friedrich Schiller's *Ode to Joy*. I would suggest that particularly the opening stanza to the *Ode to Joy*, is, in fact, reflective of this Promethean conception. It begins, "Joy, Thou beauteous Godly lightning."

And what does the joy of the fire of creative reason produce?

> Thy enchantments bind together,
> What did custom stern divide,
> Every man becomes a brother,
> Where thy gentle wings abide.

What better expression do you have of a win-win perspective? What better expression of promoting the general welfare, not only of one's own country, but of the human species? That's what Schiller puts forward there. That's the symphony that Beethoven, throughout much of his life, had wanted to compose, because he was motivated by the love of mankind, and by a will

Library of Congress

Ludwig van Beethoven

to do good, despite his ailment. Can you think of a bigger ailment for a musician to have, than not to be able to hear, to be deaf? And yet, he continued. He triumphed morally. He wasn't motivated by money, as he himself said, but by Virtue, and he produced the *Ninth Symphony*, an extraordinary, Promethean statement on behalf of all mankind.

I'll conclude at this point, because what I wanted to get at is this underlying principle behind LaRouche's Four Laws. We have to be motivated on this level if we're going to be successful in destroying the false axiomatic assumptions which control us and much of the world—the Anglo-Dutch liberal system, which unfortunately has taken over much of the thinking in the United States, for a considerable period of time. We have to destroy that, and we have to be able to recreate man, in the living image of the Creator: We have to have that kind of a Renaissance.

We're talking about new physical principles, on the one hand, as LaRouche said, and what does that mean? It means transforming the biosphere from the standpoint of what Vernadsky called the "noösphere." That means developing fusion power, a new platform altogether. It's not about merely filling potholes, or repairing roads, or building railroads *per se*. It is about developing a new economic and cultural platform, and doing that repeatedly, throughout the future, with new platforms, once the old platform has reached its limit. That's the fundamental issue which is before us.

And so, when you organize, you can't just organize for Glass-Steagall. You have to organize for the broader Renaissance conception. That's the perspective that we have to have. And if we have that perspective, this is going to be a wondrous year. We will defeat the British coup against the Presidency, we will enact Lyndon LaRouche's Four Laws, and we will join the World Land-Bridge. We will become truly man, a life-giving spirit.

II. The Four-Power Agreement

China, Japan, and the New Silk Road—Overcoming Geopolitics

by Mike Billington

May 20—A world-changing event took place last week in Japan, but anyone in the Western world who depends on the establishment press would have no way of knowing it even happened. Chinese Premier Li Keqiang visited Japan, first for a trilateral summit with Prime Minister Shinzo Abe and South Korean President Moon Jae-in (the first such trilateral summit in nearly three years), then for a series of bilateral events with Prime Minister Abe.

Historic agreements were reached between the two economic powers (Japan and China are the second and third largest economies in the world), to initiate joint investments in infrastructure projects in nations along the Belt and Road, to cooperate in joint research and development of new technologies, and to establish a cross-departmental committee to enter into an "era of coordination rather than competition," as Prime Minister Abe put it. Those in the West who are desperate to maintain the British imperial division of the world into hostile blocs, East vs. West, are chewing the rug over this historic development, and making sure it goes generally unreported in the West.

Xinhua/Li Tao

Chinese Premier Li Keqiang, Japanese Prime Minister Shinzo Abe, and South Korean President Moon Jae-in (left to right) meet the press after the 7th China-Japan-South Korea leaders' meeting in Tokyo, Japan, May 9, 2018.

Throughout the Cold War, Japan was treated by the Anglo-American "free world" as a bulwark against "Godless Communism" in Asia, both in regard to China and to Russia, while serving as a military base for the U.S. colonial wars in Indochina. Efforts by Japanese leaders, including the efforts of the grandfather and the father of the current Prime Minister Shinzo Abe (Nobusuke Kishi, Prime Minister from 1957-1960, and Shintaro Abe, Foreign Minister from 1982-1986) to establish better relations with Russia were quashed by Anglophile American leaders such as John Foster Dulles, in defense of the Cold War division of the world into enemy blocs.

Under Prime Minister Kakuei Fukuda in 1972 (as Nixon was making his famous trip to China), China and Japan established trade relations, and soon thereafter diplomatic relations. In 1978, the two nations signed a Treaty of Peace and Friendship, with China giving up demands for war reparations from Japan, and Japan recognizing One China with Beijing as its capital, and with Taiwan an integral part of China. The Taiwan issue was particularly crucial in this relationship because Japan had occupied Taiwan from 1895, following the First Sino-Japanese War, until Japan's 1945 defeat in World War II.

Following these agreements, trade and investment between the two nations skyrocketed in the 1970s, but political tensions continued to fester, because of Japan's conduct during its brutal invasion and occupation of much of China during World War II, and also because of conflicting territorial claims to islands in the East China Sea. Recurring crises involving these issues restricted political ties, and prevented a softening of the popular anger in both populations against each other. The fact that this historic distrust and animosity is finally being resolved is demonstrated by the massive increase in Chinese tourists traveling to Japan—in 2011, only 1.04 million Chinese visited Japan, but by 2017 it was 7.35 million.

Abe was elected Prime Minister for the first time in 2006, and, although he was in office for only one year due to health problems, he and his successor Yasuo Fukuda (the Son of Kakuei Fukuda) took measures to improve relations with China, such that by 2008, China and Japan were the world's largest trading partners, while Japan became the largest foreign investor in China, and still is today.

But it has been under Abe's second term as Prime Minister, which began in 2012, that major changes have taken place in respect to political relations with China, and Russia, as well. In both cases, it has required that Japan stand up to British imperial interests demanding

Yasuo Fukuda in October 2004.

that Japan follow their dictates. Abe has not shied away from this challenge, as he has long recognized that Japan's future depends on its participation in the emerging Chinese economic dynamo and in cooperation with Russia in the development of the vast frontier of Russia's Far East.

Abe and Putin

Following the U.S./British coup in Ukraine in 2014, deposing the elected government through a violent "color revolution," with neo-nazi organizations on the front lines, President Obama called Abe, demanding that he join in the condemnation of Russia for supporting those who resisted the coup, and to go along with the other G-7 nations in imposing sanctions on Russia. Abe deflected the pressure by imposing minor and meaningless sanctions, while continuing to build positive relations with Russia.

In May, 2016, Abe visited Russian President Putin in Sochi, despite a personal call from Obama instructing him not to go. Abe presented Putin with an eight-point plan for Japanese cooperation with Russia in infrastructure, health, energy, and more, both in the Russian Far East and across Russia. They also agreed to begin joint development of two of the four contested islands north of Hokkaido, including investments and visits from Japanese citizens, aiming at an eventual peace treaty to officially end World War II, through an equitable solution to the territorial issues.

Abe then attended the Eastern Economic Forum in Vladivostok in September 2016, proposing 18 development projects in the Russia's Far East. That was followed by Putin's visit to Japan in December, where 60 joint development projects were signed, totaling $2.5 billion.

Abe will be attending the St. Petersburg International Economic Forum on May 25—the first time a sitting Prime Minister of Japan has attended this annual event. He will speak on a panel at the plenary session with President Putin, French President Macron, and IMF Managing Director Christine La-

Russian President Vladimir Putin (left) with Japanese Prime Minister Shinzo Abe in Nagato, Japan, Dec. 15-16, 2016.

ogy, capital, and engineering capacities to open up fourth countries and foster rapid development across Asia.

Of course, North Korea is an obvious "+X" in this process, if the current diplomatic breakthrough in North Korean relations with President Moon and with President Trump, with major help from China, succeeds in ending the sanctions. Also, such cooperation need not be limited to Asia, but could rapidly expand to Southwest Asia and Africa, where all three Asian powers have considerable experience in building infrastructure, as well as industrial and agricultural capacities.

garde. Abe and Putin will also hold a bilateral summit on May 26, and then celebrate the "Year of Japanese-Russian Cultural Relations" with a visit to the Bolshoi Ballet.

Western "fake news" coverage of these developments has usually described them as an effort by Japan to build relations with Russia as a hedge against the "threat" of a rising China. Abe and Li Keqiang have now proven that to be a neocon pipe dream.

The New Silk Road in East Asia

All of the historic developments taking place across East Asia today, including the amazing process taking place on the Korean Peninsula, must be seen from above, as an expression of the "new paradigm" globally set in motion by Xi Jinping's Belt and Road Initiative. At the trilateral Summit between Moon, Li, and Abe on May 9 in Tokyo, they agreed to foster joint development projects in Asia in infrastructure, industrial capacity, poverty reduction, and innovation cooperation, within the framework of "China-Japan-South Korea + X." At the Summit Li Keqiang said that the Belt and Road Initiative is creating new opportunities for cooperation among the three countries, and that considering the advanced level of development of the three nations, and the development deficit in other parts of Asia, they should cooperate to bring technol-

Following the trilateral summit, Premier Li and Prime Minister Abe attended a ceremony marking the 40th anniversary of the signing of the 1978 Treaty of Peace and Friendship between China and Japan. Li called for "new steps" to bolster the confidence of the Chinese and Japanese people, as well as that of the international community, adding that the two nations should "cherish the hard-won momentum of improvement in relations."

In attendance at the ceremony was former Prime Minister Yasuo Fukuda, whose father Kakuei Fukuda had established diplomatic relations between China and Japan in the 1970s. Also in attendance was Sadayuki Sakakibara, the head of the Japanese Business Federation (Keidanren), who called for the business sectors of the two countries to collaborate "within the context of the Belt and Road."

Will President Trump succeed in bringing the United States into friendly and collaborative relations with both China and Russia, as he intends to do, even though his intention is under attack by the underlings of the British Empire? He will find full support from a united Asia if he does—an Asia which has become the core driver for the world economy, while it is forging a new kind of relationship between world powers, based on the common aims of Mankind.

New Italian Government Could Become a Game Changer

by Claudio Celani

May 22—If the new Italian government being formed by the "populist" M5S and Lega parties actually comes into being, it may upset the apple cart in Europe, even if its anti-EU positions have been watered down due to pressures from the EU, conveyed by Italy's President Sergio Mattarella. The "Contract for a Government of Change" signed by the two leaders, Luigi Di Maio and Matteo Salvini, calls for changes in foreign and economic policies which, if implemented, would break EU geopolitical schemes and throw a monkey wrench into the EU austerity regime.

Luigi Di Maio

Matteo Salvini

The contract characterizes Russia as a "potentially ever more relevant economic and commercial partner" and calls for lifting sanctions. As for Brussels, it proposes to "review the powers of the EU to return to the member countries those powers that cannot be effectively managed at the level of the Union."

On the economic side, it recommends budget flexibility and a national investment bank, and last but not least, banking separation: "We must go towards a system in which the retail credit bank and the investment bank are separated, both as concerns their type of activity and as concerns supervision."

This is the first time that bank separation ("Glass-Steagall") is part of a government program. Both the Lega and the M5S, indeed, had Glass-Steagall in their election programs and as many as 132 elected representatives, both nationally and locally—mostly Lega members but also a few M5S representatives—have signed a petition for Glass-Steagall launched in 2017 by the Italian LaRouche movement.

Implementing Glass-Steagall would be the single act of government that can finish off the global financial casino which is cannibalizing the real economy. However, for Italy as a member of the EU to do that, means violating the EU Law that establishes the universal bank as the only permitted model of chartered bank, and would amount to exiting the EU or forcing a change in the Treaty. It is not to be expected that this government will decide to wage a frontal attack on that. They have made it clear, though, that if they must take a vital decision for Italian interests, they won't hesitate to violate budget-deficit rules.

Because of that and their stated Russian-friendly foreign policy, EU officials have started to issue warnings and threats. EU deputy Commission head Valdis Dombrovskis started May 14 by urging Italy to reduce its debt. "It is clear that the approach to building the new government and towards financial stability must be to stay on the current course, gradually reducing the deficit and public debt," Dombrovskis said.

Then, on May 20, French Finance Minister Bruno Le Maire said that if Italy's commitments on "debt, deficit and bank consolidation" are not kept, "the entire stability of the Eurozone is threatened." He was followed by European People's Party faction leader Manfred Weber, who said that Italian populists are "playing with fire" with Italy's debt, and EU Trade Commissioner Cecilia Manstroem, who said that "there are worrisome things" in the Italian government program.

Among the media, London's *Financial Times* outdid everyone by headlining that "Rome opens its gates to the modern barbarians."

"Better barbarians than slaves," Lega head Salvini answered. As to the threats coming from the EU, he calmly said that "We will go to Brussels and negotiate. We are not Greece. We have a larger negotiating power, and greater economic strength than other countries." M5S Foreign Policy speaker Manlio Di Stefano told the *Financial Times* that "the barbarians have ruled Italy for the last 30 years," while M5S leader Di Maio stated that we "will demand margins to be able to spend as the second largest manufacturing power, which pays 20 billion [to the EU] and gets 10-12 back."

Sen. Alberto Bagnai, a progressive economist who joined the Lega in order to carry out his pro-independence fight, explained in a radio interview: "We do not want to make war against anyone, either the European Central Bank or Europe. We simply want to put our country in condition to recover and fulfill its potential." This would be in the interest not only of Italy, but all of Europe, he explained, because forcing countries such as Italy "to operate below its capacities, is doomed to fail."

Bagnai, who is the majority speaker on the (current) government's draft budget law, is also campaigning for the Belt and Road. Speaking in Sardinia May 17, at a rally for the coming regional elections, he said: "Sardinia has an opportunity in global developments. It has a central position in the Mediterranean which makes it an extremely important logistical hub. And therefore, we must negotiate with the EU—but maybe, first of all with ourselves—a certain new way of dealing with the fact that new routes from the East to the West—the famous Belt and Road, what they call New Silk Road— find important terminals, for instance, in this region too. And this would be a way to help strengthen its development." Bagnai is convinced that industry must be in the

Sen. Alberto Bagnai (center) with the author (left) and Prof. Enzo Pennetta in Modena, 2017.

center of economic development, but industrial and research centers can profit from the Belt and Road logistics.

Italy will not leave the euro under the new government, but the EU integration schemes pushed by Jean-Claude Juncker, Mario Draghi, Emmanuel Macron and Angela Merkel are as good as dead.

That is the good news. The bad news is that the program of the new Italian government contains several propositions which reflect the strong influence of the anti-growth and anti-scientific faction among the M5S leadership. Thus, although an earlier call to suspend the Turin-Lyon high-speed railway connection, which is in an advanced stage of construction, has been removed from the final version of the program, the program nevertheless contains a call for "reviewing" the Turin-Lyon as well all other large infrastructure projects. And M5S leaders are telling their followers that they will indeed stop such projects.

The Turin-Lyon connection is part of the strategically important Corridor 3 of the Trans-European Networks, connecting Madrid to Budapest through Northern Italy. Without that connection, which upgrades old and slow rail lines, Italy will miss a crucial connection to the Belt and Road Initiative which Sen. Bagnai indicated is in its strategic interest. In fact, while investments have begun in order to upgrade the ports of Genoa and Venice-Trieste as terminals for the Maritime Silk Road, Corridor 3 will connect those two ports to France and to Eastern Europe.

Infrastructure is the main issue of conflict between the two government partners, Lega and M5S. It is hoped that the anti-growth, other-directed faction is contained.

To Escape an Intractable World Situation? A Completely New Paradigm of Thinking!

by Helga Zepp-LaRouche, chairwoman of the German political party
Civil Rights Movement Solidarity (*BüSo*)

May 18—The number of increasingly complex and directly or indirectly related crises is on the rise: after the U.S. embassy's transfer to Jerusalem, the Israeli army's murderous crackdown on Palestinian demonstrators in the Gaza Strip, and military strikes against Hamas institutions, the worst-case scenario would be a war between Israel and Iran, which has the potential to spread further. At the same time, the hopeful perspective of a peaceful solution to the Korean crisis was torpedoed by National Security Advisor John Bolton with his provocative reference to the Libyan model as a blueprint for North Korea. The unilateral cancellation of the nuclear deal with Iran by the Trump administration naturally has an effect on North Korea; and the potential secondary sanctions against European companies operating in Iran, in addition to those affected by Russia's sanctions, threaten to trigger an escalation of the spiral of sanctions and further shatter the trans-Atlantic relationship—and above all this, hangs the sword of Damocles of a new trans-Atlantic financial crash, the "ticking time bomb" of the derivatives, of which Pope Francis now also warns in a new document.

In the case of the North Korea situation, it is difficult to believe it was just a blunder by Bolton: After the very successful summit between the presidents of North and South Korea in Panmunjom on April 27 and the equally productive visit of U.S. Secretary of State Pompeo to Pyongyang, the outlook was very good for the planned summit between President Trump and President Kim Jong-un on June 12. Bolton's assertion that the Trump administration's policy towards North Korea follows the Libya model—knowing that the entire purpose of Kim Jong-un's nuclear weapons program was to avoid the fate of Saddam Hussein and Qaddafi—had the effect of a grenade, as one might expect.

Bolton was apparently referring to the 2003 agreement, in which Qaddafi gave up his nuclear weapons program, still in its initial phases, while Trump was more likely referring to the NATO intervention in 2011, which ended with Qaddafi's assassination by U.S.-backed rebels. But Trump's correction of Bolton's statement, saying that the Libya model is only an option if North Korea does not give up its nuclear program, is unlikely to restore confidence, particularly in combination with the planned U.S.-South Korean military maneuvers three weeks before the planned summit—which, while somewhat reduced in scope, are still taking place. The way this affair developed is typical of

Xinhua

U.S. Secretary of State Mike Pompeo (left) with North Korean leader Kim Jung-un.

the way in which attempts are still being made to force Trump into the establishment's agenda.

Whether one can trust the United States to adhere to its concluded treaties is one of the most debated issues of the day, given the unilateral termination of the nuclear deal with Iran. It was only in 2017 that the Washington National Security Archive released new documents dating from the end of the Soviet Union, which clearly demonstrate that clear commitments were made to Soviet leader Gorbachev at that time "not to move NATO one inch to the east," as then Secretary of State James Baker had expressed it. But unlike Baker, Trump is not a neoconservative, in fact he won the election against the American establishment, and he has pledged to replace the canceled Iran deal with a better one. But what would such an agreement have to look like to represent an actual solution for the situation in Southwest Asia?

Sanctions Warfare and Countermeasures

Another aspect of this interconnected and complicated situation is the threat of sanctions against European companies that have invested in or are doing business with Iran. The EU is now engaged in a counter-offensive to activate the "blocking statute" adopted in 1996, a law prohibiting entrepreneurs from EU countries from submitting to unilaterally imposed U.S. sanctions. For example, if a company withdraws from its business in Iran in order to avoid being prosecuted in the United States if it is also active there at the same time, it would have to expect legal consequences from the EU. German and other European companies are also under tremendous pressure, as a result of the recent, unilateral U.S. sanctions imposed on Russia on April 6.

Trump has virtually no influence on these sanctions, and his constitutional right to formulate U.S. foreign policy was taken away from him by an earlier Senate vote that overruled his veto. However, this is never reported by the mainstream media, but instead exploited in the daily anti-Trump propaganda.

These sanctions hit around 60% of all Russian companies. Thus, e.g., Rusal, the aluminum concern of Russian oligarch Oleg Deripaska, which is on this list, accounts for nearly 40% of the primary aluminum processed in Europe. Within about ten days, the price of aluminum on the world market rose by almost 30%, forcing a cutback for a number of companies. Russia, on the other hand, began to take countermeasures by imposing sanctions on companies that comply with American or generally foreign sanctions. German Minister of Economics Peter Altmeier voiced extreme criticism of the "blocking statute" activated by EU Commission President Juncker, which he fears could lead to a "race for sanctions." Chancellor Angela Merkel, for her part, warned against any illusions that the affected companies could be financially compensated.

The new U.S. ambassador in Berlin, Richard Grenell, had been in office for only a few hours before issuing an order, in the manner of an imperial governor, for German companies to withdraw immediately from Iran. And Sandra Oudkirk, head of the U.S. Department of Energy Resources Bureau, made it clear that the United States will do everything possible to prevent the construction of the Nordstream II gas pipeline from Russia to Europe. She promised that the United States would use all of its powers of persuasion. Despite the show of confrontation against Trump, EU leaders at the recent Sofia summit in Bulgaria rushed to offer the United States accelerated imports of liquefied gas from slate fracking, which of course is being developed as an alternative to natural gas supplies from the Nordstream II pipeline.

Another geopolitical theme of the Sofia-EU summit was how to prevent the West Balkan countries from pursuing their economic and political interests via closer links with Russia, China and Turkey.

Xinhua

Chinese State Councilor and Foreign Minister Wang Yi (right front) and French Foreign Minister Jean-Yves Le Drian (left front) proceeding to their meeting in Paris, France, May 16, 2018.

A New Paradigm Reflecting the Character of Humanity

Given this seemingly intractable situation, which can only be outlined here in brief: Is there any possibility of a solution, any path that does not necessarily lead to a major Western war against Russia and China? Certainly no such approach was offered at the recent EU summit in Sofia, where the geopolitically motivated position held that the countries of the Western Balkans must absolutely be prevented from orienting towards Russia and Turkey (*author's note:* and of course China).

As Lyndon LaRouche emphasized many years ago, we can only overcome the confusing jungle of various geopolitical games by establishing a higher level of the common goals of humankind, on which the world's most important nations, especially the United States, China, Russia and India, can work together. Therefore, the announced summit between Trump and Putin is the most urgent step to tackle the numerous crises. As Chinese Deputy Prime Minister and State Councilor Liu He emphasized on his recent visit to Washington, the close personal friendship between Trump and Xi Jinping is of paramount importance. The close strategic partnership between Russia and China and the first

steps towards reorienting India towards China are further building blocks for overcoming geopolitics.

The key to overcoming all the crises mentioned here—from North Korea and Southwest Asia to the threat of trade and sanctions wars and the threat of a new financial crash—lies in the cooperation of European nations and the United States with China's New Silk Road Initiative. As Chinese Foreign Minister Wang Yi has just said in a joint press conference with his French colleague Le Drian, the volume of trade in this initiative has exceeded $4 trillion in just under five years since its inception. "Given the international situation, which is characterized by uncertainty, the Economic Belt Initiative offers a new path for common development and prosperity, and has demonstrated tremendous momentum and prospects of success," Wang Yi said.

The idea of the New Silk Road is deliberately designed to overcome geopolitical rivalries and replace them with cooperation for mutual benefit. Very much, perhaps everything, will depend on whether there are enough people in Europe and the United States who can rid themselves of the idea that politics is always a zero-sum game in which one party wins and the other loses. We will only have a positive future if we usher in a new era of international cooperation that reflects the character of humanity as the only known creative species.

zepp-larouche@eir.de

British Push Mideast Wars To Derail Emerging Four-Power Cooperation

This is the edited transcript of the May 17, 2018 Schiller Institute New Paradigm webcast, an interview with the founder of the Schiller Institutes, Helga Zepp-LaRouche. She was interviewed by Harley Schlanger. A video *of the webcast is available.*

Harley Schlanger: Hello. I'm Harley Schlanger from the Schiller Institute. Welcome to this week's international webcast, featuring our founder and President, Helga Zepp-LaRouche.

Over the last weeks Helga has been emphasizing the deployment by British imperial geopolitical interests out to wreck the promising potential that's emerged in

Eurasia, and especially the potential of a peace agreement with North Korea. Helga has repeatedly emphasized that these wrecking operations look a lot like sleepwalking into World War I. The events that just took place in Gaza in the last couple of days, the massacre there by Israeli soldiers, the threat for the situation to break out of control, all look potentially like a pre-war kind of deployment to disrupt the emergence of a four-power agreement among the nations of China, India, Russia, and the United States.

Helga Zepp-LaRouche: Yes, I think what has happened in Gaza in the last days is really a tragedy. It coincided with the opening of the U.S. Embassy in Jerusalem that I think was an unnecessary and provocative thing to do. But the situation in the Gaza is an open-air jail. It's a new Warsaw Ghetto. I'm not excluding that there are some violent Hamas elements in the midst of many Palestinians, who are rightly upset about the conditions there. This is a very tiny area. It's

the size of the small city-state of Bremen in Germany. Two million people have been crowded together in this very small area. They have no money for food; they have only a few hours of electricity a day; they have no clean water and no medical supplies. After 61 people were shot and killed, and 2,700 wounded, the already bad conditions have turned into a real nightmare, because of the inability to treat all the wounded.

People have been holding protest demonstrations. The Israeli IDF and special snipers shot into the mostly Palestinian crowd. That was completely unnecessary. If you want to dissipate a crowd, you can use water cannons or other means—you don't have to shoot and kill people. So, this brutality has inflamed the situation. Now, after a day of mourning and funerals, the confrontations are not stopping. The Israelis are making air strikes on Hamas installations in Gaza.

This could easily lead to an escalation, even to war between Israel, and Hamas and Hezbollah, and poten-

Xinhua/Wissam Nassar

Palestinian protesters carry an injured man on a stretcher, during protests in which Israeli forces shot and killed 61 people on April 6.

tially Iran. From there it could become a large-scale war. This is a terrible situation. I should remind people of the larger scope of what is happening in this area. Under the 1993 Oslo Agreement, the Palestinians were supposed to get 25% of the territory of Palestine, and the Israelis 75%. But in the meantime, 60% of the West Bank of Jordan has been occupied by Israeli settlers, so there's only 40% left. This is really becoming a very dire situation, and obviously the aim—and several people have said this—is to demoralize the Palestinians in such a way that they give up and just quit, which won't happen.

The Jewish population is rapidly becoming a minority in Israel and you cannot maintain minority rule over a hostile population that outnumbers you. We have seen that problem in other locations, such as in South Africa. It didn't function there, and it will not function here.

So even if you don't have an escalation to a big war, you have Hell! I have been saying this, and my husband has been saying it for decades: *You need economic development.* There are a lot of young people in Gaza and elsewhere, who are growing up, and who, by the age of 14, 15, and 16 feel they have no future. A chain of violence is being virtually pre-programmed.

We have been making the point for some time. While there are Christian fundamentalists in the United States who think that an early Middle East war is a good thing—I have heard such talk from those kinds of people—the reality is that the Middle East, and all of Southwest Asia, has long been the playground of British Imperialism (and at a certain point also French Imperialism). This region has been used for proxy wars by those geopolitical interests. This was demonstrated in the Sykes-Picot Treaty of 1916, which carved up this region, purposely creating the seed of future conflicts. It is now very clear that the aim is to get a confrontation with Russia—yes, with Iran—but the real target is Russia and China, to prevent the possibility of worldwide cooperation in a New Paradigm.

My husband has emphatically said many times (in speeches at many international forums) that the only way to break this terrible nightmare of violence and horror is by having a Four-Power agreement among the United States, Russia, China, and India. That way, and only that way, will you have enough people and enough

Xinhua/Khaled Omar

A Palestinian family sits outside its shack in the southern Gaza Strip, in March 2016.

military, political, and economic power to end the British Empire and therefore its ability to manipulate these situations.

A Four-Power Agreement has to be put on the agenda, because if it's not, the danger is, that this thing spirals out of control. It is already a terrible nightmare and a tragedy for the people who are suffering.

Schlanger: You mentioned the Sykes-Picot Agreement that is a perfect example of the British geopolitical deployment that led first to World War I and then in the immediate period afterwards, the British moved to try to replace the collapsing Ottoman Empire and establish what the British call the "Middle East" today, a bridge that they could control between Asia, Africa, and Europe.

These geopoliticians are on the march, they're threatening,— in Israel, you have threats against Lebanon, and Israeli strikes on Iranian positions in Syria. Helga, I think the important thing for people to understand, is your emphasis and your husband's emphasis on a bigger-picture agreement, which would be that of the great powers. None of these small states can maneuver effectively in this situation. How could such an agreement come about? Isn't this a perfect opportunity for Trump and Putin to get together, sit down, and work something out?

Zepp-LaRouche: Yes. They have already verbally agreed on having an early summit. President Trump even invited Putin to come to the White House despite the extremely difficult factional situation in the United States created by the anti-Trump, Russiagate coup attempt. That coup attempt is largely falling apart, but it's still not yet shut down. It needs to be settled by putting the perpetrators of this coup on trial instead.

Given these difficult and complex situations, if a summit between Putin and Trump were to take place as quickly as possible, and the two leaders took all the time needed to discuss and develop flanks to the situation, I think that is the one thing that could cut through all of this and create new options. I think we should all speak out and do whatever we can to ensure that such an early summit does occur.

The Underlying Threat of Financial Blowout

Schlanger: We also see the great potential on the Korean Peninsula, though somewhat set back by these unfortunate comments from National Security Advisor John Bolton, who compared North Korea to Libya. For any North Korean, this is a reminder of the fact that Muammar Qaddafi agreed to get rid of Libya's nuclear weapons and then less than a decade later, Obama, Cameron, Sarkozy and Hillary Clinton went in and destroyed Libya.

What's your sense of where things stand now, following the statement from North Korea of the cancellation of the North Korea/South Korea summit that was supposed to take place May 16? What's your sense of where this is heading?

Zepp-LaRouche: I think it is in an unstable phase, fraught with danger. It's not yet hopeless, because after this North Korea/South Korea meeting was cancelled, the U.S. State Department said the United States still assumes that the summit between Trump and Kim Jong-un will take place on June 12 in Singapore. And there were rumors in the Japanese papers that maybe even Xi Jinping would participate in such a summit. So this summit is not yet off the table. The First Vice-Minister of Foreign Affairs of North Korea, Kim Kye-gwan, drew a very clear distinction between the statements of Bolton, and those of U.S. Secretary of State Mike Pompeo and President Trump. When Pompeo returned from North Korea, he reported very respectfully and very positively about Kim Jong-un, and Trump clearly has taken up a very respectful tone towards Kim Jong-un as well. Kim Kye-gwan made this distinction very clearly. I don't know if Bolton was just being not very sharp or if he made the Libya comparison deliberately.

Gage Skidmore

National Security Advisor John Bolton.

I have no way of knowing. But for Bolton to tell the North Koreans that Kim Jong-un should follow the Libya model of denuclearization! That is the worst possible example to hold up. Soon after Qaddafi had turned over all of Libya's nuclear weapons, he was overthrown and killed. The country has been in complete chaos ever since that murder of Qaddafi, and is basically ungovernable to the present day.

The North Korean deputy foreign minister, Kim Kye-gwan, said North Korea will never accept such a model. He stressed that North Korea is talking about entering agreements not as a sign of weakness, but in an effort by Kim Jong-un to solve a very untenable, terrible situation, but not from a position of weakness. A solution cannot be accomplished by unilateral commands from the United States, but it has to unfold in a trustful atmosphere of dialogue and cooperation. I think that President Trump is intending to do that. I don't think the Kim Jong-un and Trump summit is completely at risk, but there are clearly clouds on the horizon.

The events in the Middle East are also having a peripheral impact. Think about the problem raised by many people: If the United States can rip apart its nuclear agreement with Iran, which was a negotiated agreement that took 12 years, with many nations involved, and the United Nations approved it, then such behavior casts doubt on the reliability of the United States, in general, to hold to its agreements.

All of this means we are in a very dangerous situation. There was just a new poll taken in Russia, showing that 57% of those polled were convinced that the crisis in Syria could lead to global war. I hope that war will not happen, but we are most certainly living in an atmosphere full of worry about war. People who are concerned about this should help us mobilize to bring together the concrete, viable alternative. That alternative is win-win cooperation among nations that can outflank and defeat the geopolitical agenda of war. The potential clearly is there. A lot of good things have happened: The rapprochement between China and Japan; careful steps in a similar direction between China and India; and an improvement in relations between Japan and Russia. Trump has stated his intention to keep, despite all trade issues, a good relationship with "his friend Xi Jinping," as he always calls him. And then there is the pending summit between Trump and Putin.

All the potentials are there, but it is also clear that as the Western financial system is in absolute mortal danger of a new blowout, the inherent risks facing the world cannot be overstated. Fostering every possible intervention in the direction of solving these problems with the Four Laws proposed by my husband, Lyndon LaRouche, becomes extremely urgent. So, I call on all of you to get in touch with us, become a member of the Schiller Institute, and work with us to put the Four Laws of Lyndon LaRouche before the public and on every agenda, because these measures are not only needed in the United States, they're equally needed in Europe and all other nations affected by the rotting trans-Atlantic financial system.

Between Two Paradigms: From Iran to Ukraine

Schlanger: This highlights the difficulty of existing in between two paradigms: On the one hand you have the old geopolitical, unilateralist, imperial paradigm of war, of proxy wars, of false flag attacks, of terrorism, of bail-outs, of austerity. That old paradigm is being rejected by most of the world's people and nations. But we haven't yet seen the full consolidation of the New Paradigm, and that's what the work of the Schiller Institute has been from the beginning, to bring this New Paradigm into existence.

The Iran situation seems to be hanging between these two paradigms; it's not clear where that's going. Helga, there has been some discussion among Europeans as to whether or not the Iran nuclear agreement can be salvaged. What do you know about that?

Zepp-LaRouche: Iran's Foreign Minister, Moham-

European Union foreign policy chief Federica Mogherini (right), meeting with Iranian Foreign Minister Javad Zarif in Brussels, May 15, 2018.

mad Javad Zarif, recently traveled to China and Russia, and then to Brussels, because all of these countries— that is, Russia, China, Germany, France, and Great Britain, and the EU, have stated that they want to use all possible means to maintain the Iran nuclear agreement, even though the United States has pulled out unilaterally. It is not yet clear whether that will function. The fact that Russia and China want to continue the agreement with Iran is very important.

However, should the United States insist on imposing secondary sanctions on European firms that do business with Iran, I don't know what will happen. The European Union representative, Federica Mogherini, said that, in order to protect such firms from sanctions, the EU would like to revert to certain regulations that were in place in the 1990s, but were never used. I have a hard time imagining how that would work, given that the major banks all operate internationally. Should the United States impose secondary sanctions, that act could cause absolute havoc everywhere.

The Europeans are now demanding additional negotiations with Iran; this time, however, not concerning merely Iran's nuclear program, but also the Iranian missile program, something President Trump had mentioned, in the context of saying that he would come up with a better deal. Well, I hope his better deal is a *comprehensive solution* for the whole region.

We have discussed this many times, but I want to reiterate it: If you want to solve the problems in the Middle East or Southwest Asia, you have to take into account the security interests of every single country and every single party, and that emphatically includes not only Israel, but it includes Iran, it includes the Palestinians; it includes every country. Equally important, you need to have economic development. Right now several situations are turning into nightmares. One of them is in Yemen, where *the* largest humanitarian catastrophe of the planet is now taking place. Then there is the Gaza Strip, and all the other areas that have been destroyed by these never-ending wars. Afghanistan remains quite out of control, despite some hopeful signs that this could be turned around.

In all of these quite complex situations that have been subject to terrorism, to many wars, there is widespread, deep emotional pain and scars—including an incredible accumulated rage. You need a very large-scale set of solutions. The only way to achieve that is for all of the neighboring nations—Russia, China, India, Iran, and Egypt, along with the United States, and hopefully European nations—to agree to extend the New Silk Road into the region and develop every country under a single, integrated, industrial infrastructure development program.

There are already the beginnings of that. Three years ago, when President Xi Jinping was in Iran, he agreed with President Hassan Rouhani that the New Silk Road would be extended into Iran. Afghanistan's President has demanded that the New Silk Road be applied in Afghanistan. At their recent two-day "informal summit" in Wuhan, China, President Xi Jinping and India's Prime Minister Narendra Modi agreed that China and India would cooperate in bringing the Silk Road into Afghanistan by building, as a first step, an extensive rail connection between China and Iran through Kyrgyzstan, Tajikistan, and Afghanistan, thereby connecting Afghanistan into the Silk Road.

That same approach must be taken for Iraq, for Syria, and for Yemen. Egypt will have to play a very important role as a bridge between Asia and Africa. I think Egypt is thinking in this direction already. These are all gigantic projects that cannot be built by any one country alone. China has a special envoy for Syria: the Chinese government has said it wants to play a leading role in the reconstruction of Syria. You have the earlier

Xinhua/Ju Peng

China's President Xi Jinping (left) talks with Iranian President Hassan Rouhani in Tehran, Jan. 23, 2016.

commitment of Russia to supply energy, and of Iran to help in the industrial development. But all this needs to be presented as a comprehensive proposal.

I'm sure that there are people in Israel, as well, who do not agree with the present course of Netanyahu—who is facing his own problems and whose career may not have a bright future. There are people in Israel who do agree on the need to come out of this terrible paradigm of the present configuration. Were Trump, Xi Jinping, Putin and Modi to come to an agreement for such a big, coordinated development package, other leaders would join them, to go in this direction. Even this very difficult situation of Southwest Asia could be approached and a solution found. But it requires an extraordinary intervention.

Schlanger: To inform our new viewers, and to remind our regular viewers, we produced that very blueprint in our report, *Extending the New Silk Road to West Asia and Africa: A Vision of an Economic Renaissance*. It is available through the Schiller Institute and is a comprehensive picture of the Chinese proposals, and what they're actually already doing in coordination with plans generated by host countries, breaking new ground, creating jobs, educating people, and doing the necessary job training.

There's one other danger spot that won't go away, and that's the situation in Ukraine, where this week the Ukrainian government raided the offices of RIA Novosti, a Russian news agency; there are various kinds of threats coming from Poroshenko, and the neo-Nazis in the security agencies in Ukraine.

You also have a very interesting opening of a new bridge linking Russia with Crimea. This new bridge has caused some wild Ukrainian fascists to call for blowing it up, claiming it to be an attack on Ukrainian independence.

Helga, what's the situation on the ground as far as you can see, in Ukraine right now?

Zepp-LaRouche: The raid on the offices of RIA Novosti is very serious. RIA Novosti Ukraine bureau chief Kirill Vyshinsky was arrested. The Ukrainian government is comparing RIA Novosti with Nazi Minister of Propaganda Joseph Goebbels. In Ukraine right now, the situation is quite dire for the freedom of the press.

When German Chancellor Angela Merkel goes to Sochi, Russia to meet with Putin, this will be one of the subjects of discussion, as well as the other crisis spots. So, I think if we could somehow revive the Minsk Agreement, this would go a long way toward resolving the situation in Ukraine, because right now the Kiev government is absolutely not cooperating. Poroshenko has even signed into law a bill labeling Russia the aggressor regarding the eastern Ukraine separatist-held areas of Donetsk and Luhansk, in order to solve the situation in East Ukraine by military means. So this is definitely another extremely dangerous situation.

But, because it is so dangerous, I think more people are waking up to that, and that may be a first step to hopefully prevent something which could easily become World War III.

Russiagate Collapses, but Financial Collapse Looms

Schlanger: The Ukraine issue brings up another aspect of Russiagate. I was just doing a review of this in the last couple of days, and I noticed something that I had forgotten, which is that John Brennan, the former

Kremlin photo

Russian President Vladimir Putin at the opening ceremony for the Crimean Bridge motorway, May 15. Here, he drives the lead vehicle in a construction equipment convoy.

CIA director who is at the center of much of the operation of Russiagate against Trump, had made a secret trip to Kiev shortly after the overthrow of Ukraine's legitimately elected President, Viktor Yanukovych, and put in motion U.S. support for the criminal regime that took over. Brennan's involvement in the Robert Mueller coup attempt and what Sen. Rand Paul brought up about this becomes very important.

Helga, do you think this adds to the weight against Special Counsel Mueller? Several judges are turning against him. There are increasingly more exposés of the FBI and overall corruption. Where is all this heading?

Former CIA director John Brennan.

Forbes Washington

APR 16, 2014 @ 04:30 PM   14,286

Why CIA Director Brennan Visited Kiev: In Ukraine The Covert War Has Begun

Melik Kaylan, CONTRIBUTOR
FULL BIO

Opinions expressed by Forbes Contributors are their own.

Ukraine is on the brink of civil war, Vladimir Putin has said, and he should know because the country is already in the midst of a covert intelligence war. Over the weekend, CIA director John Brennan travelled to Kiev, nobody knows exactly why, but some speculate that he intends to open US

Why hasn't it been shut down by now?

Zepp-LaRouche: I think it could be shut down quickly, because the latest twist is that Mueller himself is now suspected of having colluded with a Russian oligarch, which I'd find a little bit humorous, if the situation weren't so serious.

But I think the letter by Sen. Rand Paul is really important. On May 15, he wrote a letter to Gina Haspel, then the Acting Director of the CIA and Trump's nominee to become Director of the Agency, demanding that she answer four questions, "particularly in relation to surveillance during the 2016 presidential election." Did the CIA bug any Presidential candidates in 2016, not just Trump, but any other candidate? Given the fact that the CIA is prohibited by law from surveilling Americans, has the CIA "ever cooperated with any foreign intelligence services to surveil, monitor, or collect any information on candidate Trump …" And, "Did the CIA or any other U.S. government agency conduct surveillance on, or engage in the collection of communications or information about then-candidate President Trump during his November 2016 visit to Great Britain?"

And then, in an interview with NBC News on the same day, he even went further, bringing up, in this context, the visit by Robert Hannigan, the former head of GCHQ, the British equivalent of the NSA, to the United States to brief then CIA Director John Brennan about all of this.

It is now coming out in the mainstream media that there was collusion with British intelligence. This is really a very good development. Such activity clearly *is* completely illegal and unconstitutional; it may be even criminal. The more quickly these things are followed up, the better.

House Intelligence Committee Chairman, Congressman Devin Nunes (R-Ca.), has said that it's now 100% certain that there was absolutely no collusion of the Trump team with Russia. Nunes asks the question: Given that those who pretended that there was such collusion knew that it did not exist, why was this whole operation instigated in the first place?

I think this question must be answered. This is an ongoing coup attempt against a duly elected President of the United States. The exposure of these coup plotters has focused a bright light on the forces of the Empire—we call it the British Empire, because it is in the continuity of the British Empire. All those who have come out so quickly against Trump on the side of those who accused Trump, have also shown their true colors.

If the United States is to return to its constitutional form, the entire FBI and Department of Justice must be cleaned out and reorganized afresh. I think all of this is necessary.

Trump must be freed from this British attack. This so-called Russiagate is the only reason the relationships with Russia, with China, have not gone forward. It is why, in an indirect form, the Middle East crises have become so dangerous. If world peace is to be saved, the British-directed coup must be fully brought to light. All the culprits must be held accountable. And then Trump can actually do what he promised he would do—and most of it actually is in the right direction. Even some of the critics have to see that.

The Damocles Sword hanging over all of us, however, is the danger of a financial blowout. We must, as an absolute priority, have a full discussion of the value of re-imposing not only Glass-Steagall, but changing over to Hamiltonian economics—applying the Four Laws, of my husband, Lyndon LaRouche.

China's Offer to India Sheds Geopolitics

Schlanger: In conclusion, Helga, I'd like to pose something to you concerning Hamiltonian economics in the context of all of these war provocations and the British pulling every string that they have. The Chinese are continuing with very bold plans around the New Silk Road. The New Silk Road Spirit, as you call it, is catching on all around the world. Even with the efforts of some to sabotage the U.S.-China relationship around trade, around tariffs, and things of that sort, the U.S.-China relationship seem to be moving in a potentially good direction, with the visit of another team of Chinese officials to Washington.

How do you think this can affect the overall situation—the Trump-Xi relationship? Isn't that really one of the keys to breaking through to the New Paradigm?

Zepp-LaRouche: Yes. Were the proposal by Li Keqiang, the Chinese Prime Minister, to be taken up, the way to balance the trade between the United States and China is not by imposing tariffs, but could be achieved in a much more elegant way, by increasing trade and investments in third countries. There are plenty of opportunities to do this: The United States could join with China in investments in Latin America, the Middle East, and other Asian countries. There is a new Chinese offer now to India, that they need not be rivals in African investment: Given that China has great expertise in building infrastructure, while India is really lagging behind in that capability, China proposes that they should join efforts, with India contributing in the areas they can do well, and China providing the large-scale infrastructure, without which none of these investments can function.

The United States could also be a part of this. To look at the world in a non-geopolitical way is, I know, almost impossible for some people to imagine, because they are so trained that the world is a zero-sum game; that there can be only a single hegemonic power; that if China rises, the United States must go under, or, in order for the United States to thrive, it must be at the expense of the rest of the world. None of that is true. China has many times made the point that it does not want to replace the United States as a unipolar, dominant force, but instead wishes to have a new type of relations among major powers. And that dramatically involves joint economic projects in third countries, joint ventures—redefining entirely how to go about it.

Look at history from a longer arc. It is not natural for people to solve conflicts with weapons or wars. This is what I have always called infantile diseases of mankind. Little boys kick each other in the shins when they are four or even seven years old. Eventually, you grow up and become an adult. You learn to cherish the creative mind of the other person and work together, like Max Planck and Einstein, like Schiller and Humboldt. You can establish relationships with people in other countries in which you address the creative potential of other people and enrich, in turn, your own potential.

Humanity is, after all, the only species capable of creative reason, of making fundamental discoveries of universal principles of the physical universe again and again, and in that way developing more knowledge about our planet, and the universe. We can continue to discover principles of science and technology that we can then apply to the production process, leading to increases in productivity, which then lead to increases in living standards and increases in longevity,—this is what we are! We are not animals. We are human beings, the only species, at least known so far to us in the universe, that can relate to our creative power as our unique identity.

If we take that approach, of having many nations, each based on the best of its several cultural traditions, all with perfect sovereignty, we can all work together toward a higher level of reason, and that is the *only* way mankind will survive! I think we are at a crossroads: If we decide to stay with geopolitics, this will lead to World War III, and, for all we know, the virtual extinction of our species. On the other hand, the New Paradigm beckons. Already, 140 countries are cooperating in improving the conditions of life for their citizens. I think we need a mass movement of people who have come to the realization that mankind has reached a new era and are willing to work together to consciously form our future, our "shared community for the future of mankind," as Xi Jinping always calls it.

Let this be the discussion we have among ourselves and with everyone we meet.

Schlanger: I think you have just made a compelling case for people to give up sleepwalking, and instead catch the New Silk Road Spirit. So, Helga, until next week. Thank you, and thank you for joining us.

To those of you who are watching this program, take up this challenge: Take up the challenge to become active with the Schiller Institute. Thank you, and see you next week.

August 9, 1996

Phil Gramm:
Not the Only Quackademic

by Lyndon H. LaRouche, Jr.

Veteran draft-avoider and quackademic Senator Phil Gramm, and House Speaker Newton Gingrich, are not the only consumer frauds rampant in university faculty lounges today. Although a small minority among today's professional economists is composed of both literate and insightful professionals, virtually everything taught as *principles of economics,* is an illiterate's hoax.

The legendary, pervasive incompetence of most leading and other campus economists, is emerging, once again, to be a timely topic of public opinion. The presently insurgent contempt for the official economists, should remind us of moods which erupted after August 15, 1971, when a global monetary collapse, which Paul Samuelson, like others, had said could never happen, triggered abandonment of the Bretton Woods gold-reserve agreements. Today, as the storms of an on-rushing international banking collapse darken the skies, we might expect, soon, that all we shall hear from under the crack in the door of the Economics Department, will be a mewling murmur: "No one here but us visiting ditch-diggers."

Those who recall the period of the 1971 monetary crisis, may also recall the face-to-face and literary debates which this writer conducted with some among the most famous U.S. economists, during the closing months of that year. Every trend which this writer then warned was likely to happen, unless policy-decisions of the 1966-1971 period were reversed, has become the ugly truth of today, inside the U.S.A., and worldwide. The mass-murderous policies of Phil Gramm, Newt Gingrich, and Pennsylvania Governor Tom Ridge, today, are the policies against which this writer, in 1971, forewarned the public, in prophetic detail, as the fascist trends implicit in 1966-1971 policies. What experience, since then, teaches, is, chiefly, that what most of today's high-ranking students of economic policy—at the ***Wall Street Journal, Washington Post,*** in the Republican Party, and Yuppiedom elsewhere— appear to have learned best from the experience of the past thirty years' economic decline of the U.S.A. and world economies, alike, is how to surpass their parents of the World War II veterans' generation, in transforming the disasters of the past into the catastrophes of the present.

Admittedly, there are important differences between the putative leading economists of 1971 and those of today. Like kitchen con-man Phil Gramm, or Newt Gingrich, most of today's populist economists tend to be low-budget imitations of such higher-priced models of Mont Pelerin clansmen as Friedrich von Hayek and Milton Friedman. Whereas the economists of the 1950s and 1960s blundered in their representation of the processes of production, Gramm and Gingrich typify those popular economists of today's mass media and foundation circuits, who have rejected any serious attempts to understand the productive process itself.

The notable point of difference is, that the thoughts of today's Yuppie economists, dwell, as byte-afflicted hesychasts, in the caves of "cyber-space." Ideologue Malthilde Ludendorff would have been greatly embarrassed to foresee, that the aging Yuppie of today, has rejected modern European civilization's traditional functional standards of physical performance, out of preference for the cultural determinists' coddling consolations of fantasy-life, those of the proverbial, twice-weekly, psychotherapy circle's Orwellian "group

Left: Sen. Phil Gramm. His mass-murderous policies are those which Lyndon LaRouche warned, in 1966-71, would emerge from the fascist trends implicit at that time. Right: The 1971 debate between Professor Abba Lerner (at microphone) and LaRouche (with bowtie). Since that time, no U.S. academic economist has been willing to risk his skin in a public debate with LaRouche.

think." It is but a reflection of this point of difference, that, for today's Generation X'er, Hannah Arendt's beloved, the leading Nazi ideologue Martin Heidegger, and other German and French, existentialist co-thinkers of Hitler-prophet Friedrich Nietzsche, are the preferred symbols of most of today's university philosophy departments.

The crucial point to be made here, is that every scrap of innovation in generally accepted classroom teaching of economics, since about 1966, must be recognized for the certifiable lunacy it is. For example: Those twin pillars of psychotic cyber-space, "information theory" and "systems analysis," must be purged, outrightly, from the policy-shaping discussions. Attention must be focussed upon correcting the prevailing errors of an earlier generation, when professional economists were more or less sane, even when in grave, axiomatic error. We must address the hereditary impact upon today's economies, of those blunders which prevailed during an earlier generation's time, when economists still lived in the real world, where physical, rather than merely financial or monetary performance, per capita, per household, and per square kilometer, were the yardsticks to which professional standards for economic-policy discussion obliged us, ultimately, to return. In that former time, monetary and financial systems were judged by the physical-economic performance they were arguably proposed to have fostered: the exact reverse of the standard employed by today's hegemonic pack of professional lunatics.

Only when we have stated the problem in such, admittedly, rude and insensitive, terms of plain speech, do we escape the prison-yard of "politically correct" babbling, into the fresh, free air, where sane men and women enjoy healthy respect for the realities urgently to be addressed.

The Abba Lerner Debate of 1971

For those who remember, and others, consider the circumstances and outcome of the writer's celebrated Autuman 1971 debate with Professor Abba Lerner, then considered the leading Keynesian economist of the United States. That turned out to be a bench-mark, a turning-point in the history of the U.S. economics profession. On that account, certain essential features of the debate are of signal importance, for understanding the leading economic policy-issues of the U.S. today.

Following the events of August 16-17, 1971, the author's associates deployed in numerous university campuses of the U.S.A., challenging the economics departments on three key points. First, that virtually all among them, had been proven incompetent by the August 16-17 events, on the principal point of their teaching to their students, up to that point in time. On this account, we described the relevant such professors of economics as "quackademics." Second, that their teaching would lead, in practice, into introducing forms of economic austerity, world-wide, against labor, and others, echoing the measures of fascistic economists such as Hjalmar Schacht, in 1920s and 1930s Germany. Third, we, as critics, were willing to meet any challenge from the accused economists, by offering the author of these two charges, the present writer, to debate publicly any champion the offended academic economists might select.

In short, the New York academic economists selected Professor Abba Lerner to be that champion. An audience of under 1,000, chiefly faculty representatives and students, attended. Throughout, this writer focussed upon the charge which he had made publicly against Lerner: that Lerner's economic theory had already impelled Lerner to propose, or to support otherwise, measures of austerity modelled upon the fascist measures imposed in 1930s Germany by Nazi Minister Hjalmar Schacht. In the end, Lerner conceded, in effect, by delivering what most in the audience heard as a shocking admission, Lerner's apology for the policies of Schacht: He stated, that had the German Social-Democracy supported Schacht, "Hitler would not have been necessary." The quotation is exact.

Afterward, Lerner's closest political associate, the noted John Dewey clansman and former Communist, Professor Sidney Hook, avowed: Yes, LaRouche had defeated Lerner in the debate, but LaRouche would pay a price for that success. On one point, Hook proved accurate: Since that time, no U.S. academic economist has been willing to risk his skin in a public debate with this writer.

Although, many among those relevant, professional economists of the post-August 1971 decades, would have rightly insisted that they were not personally fascist ideologues, the characteristic tendency of their policy-shaping always moved them in the direction of either recommending the kinds of fascistic trends in economic policy against which this writer had warned in August 1971, or making excuses for those who did so. Just as this writer had first warned, in late August 1971, the consistent trend in U.S. academic and governmental economic policy-shaping, since then, has been toward the kind of fascist austerity presently typified by either Newt Gingrich's co-thinkers, or the utterly shameless neo-Nazism of the fuzzy-tongued former Colorado governor, Reform Party pre-candidate Dick Lamm.

Thus, were Hitler alive and running as candidate of the Nazi Party in Germany—or, in the United States, today, even among most liberal academics, it would be forbidden, on grounds of "political correctness," to describe that candidate Hitler, or Pennsylvania Governor Tom Ridge, as promoting "Nazi-like" policies. Among radical conservatives, "neo" or other, in today's U.S.A., the charge of "Nazi-like," or simply "fascist," strikes too close to home for comfort. Not only arguable fascists, such as Newt Gingrich or Phil Gramm, have reason to be sensitive on this issue; most so-called "liberal" economists are carriers of the epidemic trends in thinking, not only in economics, but on social policy generally.

Go back to 1966-1971. *Why* did most liberal economists of that time, as Professor Abba Lerner typifies the case, take the first baby-steps, leading toward what should have been visible to them as today's GOPAC and kindred threats of full-blown American fascism? What was included, or perhaps missing, from their comprehension of economic processes, which has led into mass-murderous fascistic policies such as those of Gingrich's "Contract on Americans," and of the man classed variously as "apparent," or "aberrant" candidate for the Republican Party's Vice-Presidential nomination, the "Nuremberg criminal" Pennsylvania Governor Tom Ridge?

The present writer has identified this specific problem, repeatedly, within policy analyses published earlier in editions of *Executive Intelligence Review,* and other locations. We bring that issue into sharper focus upon the specific topic posed here.

Prince Philip Says He Is a 'Higher Ape'

While his wife has been otherwise occupied, the co-founder of the World Wildlife Fund, Britain's Duke of Edinburgh, Prince Philip, has insisted, repeatedly, that he is neither a man, nor a horse, but a "higher ape." As it was for Charles Darwin, since long before both the Duke and the U.S.A.'s "Unabomber," that is the kernel of neo-Malthusian philosophy, to which today's World Wide Fund for Nature is devoted; it is the kernel of the issue of economics upon which our attention is focussed here.

The characteristic feature of all physical economy,

from the most remote point of pre-history of mankind, to the present, is the increase of human potential relative population-density, from the level of several millions living individuals, the maximum for any imaginable higher ape, such as Prince Philip, to several hundred millions, and then billions, as the consequence of a succession of changes in typically human behavior, as exemplified by scientific and technological progress in both the development of inhabited areas, and in the productive powers of labor. This measurement of productive powers of labor, is expressed in terms of physical contents of market-baskets of output, and of consumption, per capita, per household, and per square kilometer of relevant land-area.

Converted into the language of classroom thermodynamics, this increase in life-expectancy, standard of living, and potential density of population, depends upon an increase of the level of the potential productivity of the imputable labor-force of society, per capita. As Gottfried Leibniz specified, in founding the science of physical economy, in his 1671 **Society & Economy,** this level of productive potential in the member of the labor-force, depends upon a corresponding standard of material and cultural existence, among the family households which produce the members of the labor-force. This also requires appropriate levels of physical improvement of basic economic infrastructure of the society taken as a whole, and increased levels of expenditure, per capita, in capital facilities, and in materials invested in the individual work-place.

Continuing to examine the history of physical economy, from earliest known times, in these same terms of reference, we have the following notable results.

Identify the aggregation of those costs (and related investments) necessary to sustain a certain level of productive powers of labor for a society, as corresponding to "energy of the system." Identify any margin of output in excess of those costs, as "free energy." Thus, we are presented with the notion of some ratio of "free energy" to "energy of the system." This ratio, as expressed in physical terms, not monetary or analogous terms, provides society a standard of measure of performance. This standard is composed of the relationship between two elements: 1) absolute "energy of the system" per capita of labor force, as measured in relative physical content of market-baskets of standard necessary consumption; 2) ratio of "free energy" to "energy of the system."

The increase of the productive powers of labor, is expressed initially, in terms of increase of the required physical content of all market-baskets: production, infrastructure, and capital investment in production. These are measured threefoldly: per capita of labor-force, per household, and per relevant square kilometer. The associated, required condition, is that the ratio of "free energy" to "energy of the system" must not decline, despite the increase (in physical terms, and as measured in terms of the division of labor) of the capital-intensity of required "energy of the system" (per capita, per household, and per square kilometer).

That latter restriction ("constraint") may be termed, conveniently, the characteristic required function of the economy considered as a whole, or, simply, *Characteristic Function.*

The commonplace, fallacious assumption, even prior to 1966-1971, was that economics must proceed from the "microcosm," as of the individual farm, factory, or trading-house, to build up to the level of considering the society as a whole.[1] For those of such opinion, thus, productivity must be measured, first, at the point of production within the individual firm, and that in respect to ratios of prices of sales versus prices of necessary purchases. The question whether the gain of the individual enterprise came as a loss to the society as a whole, was not considered. This attempt to derive a general theory of political-economy from an assumed microcosmic "cell form," was the usual situation, and is the essence of the fallacious approach taken by the followers of the British East India Company's Haileybury School, such as Adam Smith, Jeremy Bentham, Thomas Malthus, David Ricardo, Karl Marx, et al. In more recent decades, it was argued that this was the "capitalist," or "free society" approach, supposedly as distinct from the Soviet approach.

During the late 1940s through 1960s, there came an epidemic of lunacy in the military and security institutions of the U.S.A. The case of the FBI under the Hoover-Tolson dynasty is notorious. The military side of the problem is more interesting, and more directly relevant to the concerns we have expressed here. It began, as an invasion of silly varieties of so-called "social science," invading the newly created U.S. Air Force, during the late 1940s: as through RAND and MIT channels, such as those associated with Margaret Mead and her sometime husband, Gregory Bateson of MK-Ultra notoriety. During the 1960s, this plague took

---

1. As by aggregating "Value Added" of the economy's individual parts.

over West Point Military Academy. This invasion by "mind snatchers," included a strong emphasis upon the pseudo-scientific cults of "cybernetics" and "systems analysis." It spread through leading universities, and prominent military suppliers and influential "think tanks"; it was purveyed widely through the forums of the American Management Association and kindred circuits, and through the "technical" textbooks of the notorious "how to deceive your neighbors into thinking you are a genius, all in less than one hour a day, all in your spare time" variety. The notorious cult text, ***High Frontier,*** is an example of this latter sort of charlatanry.

This infusion of pseudo-science provided a medium for the spread of a hyperventilating mantra: "Free economy versus command economy." That mantra has served as the predecessor of the fascist (anti-"big government") communitarianism cult adopted by Speaker Newt Gingrich and his fellow-clansmen of "Contract on Americans" (those considered by Gingrich, Ridge, their supporters, et al. to be "useless eaters").[2] The wild-eyed fanaticism associated with that mantra, has contributed a significant part to the incompetence of taught (and practiced) economics today.

More significant than that mantra, has been the popularization of "material incentives," a doctrine whose impact upon quality is typified by a visit to any gallery offering an exhibition of what passes for modern art among the wealthy, and would-be-wealthy decadent classes of today. The same sick minds have supplied us the related dogma of "psychological" (as distinct from "material") incentives (e.g., a more resonant job-description, in lieu of a pay raise). In short, the influence of pathetic varieties of so-called "social science" upon economic policy-shaping, has been to impose a Hobbesian, morally degraded conception of "human nature," upon the practice of the firm, and the society as a whole. "Lure people into being 'more productive,' through material and other psychological incentives."

The crux of the matter is implicit in the assertion: "No amount of bananas or stroking, could induce baboons (or, perhaps, Prince Philip) to invent the wheel."

The widespread, credulous toleration of the outrageously anti-scientific, axiomatic assumptions, underlying the work of such followers of Bertrand Russell as Norbert Wiener ("information theory") and John von Neumann ("systems analysis"), exemplifies the nature of the incompetence pervading economics teaching even prior to the 1966-1971 interval, and even more so after that. Von Neumann's assumption, as set forth publicly by him in 1938, was that all economies can be reduced, for purposes of analysis, to the terms of solutions for systems of simultaneous linear inequalities. Wiener's fatal presumption, was that human intelligence could be reduced to an expression of Ludwig Boltzmann's statistical thermodynamics of a linear kinematic model, the so-called "H-theorem." The absurdity of Wiener's assumption subsumes the identical quality of foolishness in von Neumann's views of both economies and the human brain.

As we have summarized the fact, above, any successful economy must satisfy the requirement, that the productivity must be increased, through such means as emphasis upon investment in scientific and technological progress. However, although this requires an increase in the relative (physical) "energy of the system" of the economy, taken as a whole, per capita, per household, and per square kilometer, the ratio of "free energy" to "energy of the system" must not decline. That is, a true "not-entropic" process, whose very existence suffices to demonstrate that the universe, taken in its entirety, is, similarly, "not-entropic."[3] This fact has crucial economic implications; it also has, as Bernhard Riemann showed implicitly, in his 1854 habilitation dissertation, the most profound implications for both mathe-

---

2. "Communitarianism," as typified by former Columbia University denizen and Professor Amitai Etzioni, is an explicitly fascist movement derived from the Nazi Party circles' traditions met in Schumacher's ***Small is Beautiful.*** Etzioni's "communitarianism" was initially presented, during the mid-1970s, under Etzioni's rubric of "fascism with a human face." Obviously, the attack upon "big government" is part of the movement to replace national governments by UNO world government, and national economies by a single, "global economy" controlled by world government.

3. The fact, that mankind's potential relative population-density has been increased through valid, axiomatic-revolutionary discoveries of natural principle, demonstrates, the universe is prone, by its implied principle of design, to submit to the properly developed human powers of cognitive discovery of principle. Hence, the characteristic feature of that process of higher hypothesis, which subsumes a series of successful discoveries of principle, is a aaareflection of the lawful design of the universe as a whole. Since, an efficient realization of the "not-entropic" series, in economic development, expresses the mathematical form of Riemann's 1854 habilitation dissertation, and since this series is in correspondence with scientific progress, the ordering subsumed by mankind's cognitive powers for successive, valid, axiomatic-revolutionary discoveries of principle, reflects the "not-entropic" ordering-principle characteristic of the universe to which man's successful efforts at discovery are addressed. An elaboration of the principles involved will be found in the forthcoming publication of this writer's "Leibniz From Riemann's Standpoint," ***Fidelio,*** Fall 1996.

matics and mathematical-physics in general.

Whence this "not-entropic" impulse, so indispensable to the continued existence of the human species? It is derived, ultimately, from valid, axiomatic-revolutionary qualities of discovery of principles of nature, in both science and Classical art-forms. These discoveries, by their nature, can not be communicated, in the form of what Wiener presumes to be "information": by means of a mathematical or other language based upon levels of knowledge existing prior to that mental act of discovery. Such discoveries can be communicated, only by prompting a replication of the original discovery within the sovreign precincts of the individual mind of the student, et al. It is in this process of evoking reenactments of original discoveries of principle, that knowledge is imparted to the present generations from the past, and valid new discoveries of principle added to the stock of human knowledge.

As Riemann emphasizes,[4] the incorporation of any valid new principle into mathematical physics, requires us to depart the domain of mathematical formalism for the realm of experimental physics, and, thereafter, to redesign mathematics to accommodate what the old mathematics could never develop, or represent. That quality of invention, is the only source of the "not-entropy" upon which all economy depends.

In mathematical terms, the pathway of economic meta-equilibrium demanded by the characteristic function of physical economy, is described by what is known as a "Riemann Surface Function," a succession of physical geometries, ordered in terms of advances in Gaussian curvature, each employed to represent the characteristic of that stage of advancement of the economy.

Thus, for any competently designed economic policy, the following leading rules apply:

1. There must be a universal Classical form of education (e.g., the Humboldt model formerly used, for the more fortunate students, in Germany), for all young members of society. (Not merely trade-school, or other so-called "practical" education. No John Dewey, or "New Math" permitted. Lots and lots of "dead, white, European males," and others, are required for all.)

2. The standard wage-income or substitute for all households of society, must conform to the cultural level of something better than the presently desired productive potential of the labor-force.

3. The improvements in infrastructure and work-place, per capita, per household, and per square kilometer, must conform to the Characteristic Function of physical economy.

4. The rate of development of, and investment in scientific and technological progress, and in Classical cultural development, must be sufficient to satisfy, in effect, the Characteristic Function of physical economy.

The beginning of economic science is to be found in the appropriate Biblical location: *Genesis* 1:26-30. The scientific evidence is, that man and woman are made in the living image of the Creator, by virtue of that developable creative power of the human individual through which mankind's power over the universe is increased without limit. A science of economy, is the branch of physical science which premises itself upon the increase of the physical power of survival of mankind, through reliance upon the development of those creative mental powers, for valid, axiomatic-revolutionary discovery of principle, which sets humanity absolutely apart from, and above, all other creatures.

That is the essence of the matter. That, therefore, is the point of reference from which to discover the cause for any economic affliction which mankind imposes upon itself.

---

4. e.g., 1854 habilitation dissertation.